Conrad: *The Secret Agent*

Casebook Series

GENERAL EDITOR: A. E. Dyson

Conrad

The Secret Agent

A CASEBOOK

EDITED BY

IAN WATT

MACMILLAN

First published 1973 by
THE MACMILLAN PRESS LTD
London and Basingstoke
Associated companies in New York Toronto
Dublin Melbourne Johannesburg and Madras

SBN 333 04268 9 (hard cover)
    333 07987 6 (paper cover)

Printed in Great Britain by
THE ANCHOR PRESS LTD
Tiptree, Essex

CONTENTS

ACKNOWLEDGEMENTS

The editor and publishers wish to thank the following, who have kindly given permission for the use of copyright material: the Trustees of the Joseph Conrad Estate and J. M. Dent & Sons Ltd for letters by Joseph Conrad from *Joseph Conrad: Life and Letters*, edited by G. Jean-Aubry (1927); the *New Statesman and Nation* for 'Novel of the Week: *The Secret Agent*' by Edward Garnett, from *The Nation*, 28 September 1907; the Nonesuch Press Ltd for *Letters from Conrad: 1895–1924*, edited by Edward Garnett (1928); the Society of Authors as literary representatives of the Estate of John Galsworthy for 'Joseph Conrad: A Disquisition', from *Fortnightly Review*, no. 496 (1 April 1908); Martin Secker & Warburg Ltd and Alfred A. Knopf Inc. for 'Joseph Conrad's *The Secret Agent*', from *Past Masters, and Other Papers* by Thomas Mann (1933), translated in the United States by H. T. Lowe-Porter; Sir Rupert Hart-Davis for '*The Secret Agent*' by Hugh Walpole, from *A Conrad Memorial Library: The Collection of George T. Keating* (1929); Chatto & Windus Ltd and New York University Press for the extract from *The Great Tradition* by F. R. Leavis (1948); A. D. Peters & Co. and Harold Matson Co. Inc. for 'An Émigré', from *Books in General* by V. S. Pritchett © 1953; Horizon Press for the extract from 'Conrad: Order and Anarchy', from *Politics and the Novel* by Irving Howe © 1957; Harvard University Press for the extract from 'Two Versions of Anarchy', from *Conrad the Novelist* by Albert J. Guérard © 1958 Harvard University Press; Robert D. Spector and the Regents of the University of California for 'Irony as Theme: Conrad's *The Secret Agent*' by Robert D. Spector, from

Nineteenth-Century Fiction, XIII (1958) © 1958 by the Regents of the University of California; Johns Hopkins Press for 'The Symbolic World of *The Secret Agent*' by Avrom Fleishman, from *English Literary History*, XXXII (1965); Harvard University Press for '*The Secret Agent*', from *Poets of Reality* by J. Hillis Miller © 1965 Harvard University Press; Norman Sherry for 'The Greenwich Bomb Outrage and *The Secret Agent*', from *Review of English Studies*, n.s., XVIII (1967); The Bodley Head (*Return to Yesterday*), Ford Madox Ford, *Volume V* and Mrs Theodora Zavin for the extract from *Your Mirror to My Times*, ed. Michael Killigrew, published by Holt, Rinehart.

PART ONE

Critical Survey

EDITOR'S NOTE

The critical classifications attempted in Part One may serve to suggest one way of looking at the characteristic approaches of the essays which follow in Part Two, and in providing them with something of a historical context. The categories are, of course, highly simplified, and rather than impose distinctions that are always, to some extent, arbitrary, the essays below are arranged in chronological order.

All the essays are complete, except where indicated by ellipses. Double ellipses (.. ...) are used to mark an omission of a paragraph or more. No changes have been made in the text, except that the notes have been renumbered or amplified where necessary.

Page references to quotations from Conrad are uniformly to the Dent Collected Edition.

Since Part One : Critical Survey was written, a certain amount of new work on *The Secret Agent* has appeared, notably in Norman Sherry's *Conrad's Western World*. I particularly regret that considerations of length prevented the inclusion of Eloise Knapp Hay's appreciation of *The Secret Agent* in her book, *The Political Novels of Joseph Conrad*.

I. W.

1 COMPOSITION OF
THE SECRET AGENT

The first mention of *The Secret Agent* occurs in a letter from Conrad to his literary agent J. B. Pinker on 21 February 1906. Deeply exhausted by the completion of *Nostromo*, Conrad had been seriously ill at the end of 1905 and had escaped to the relative warmth of Montpellier. There he had worked on some short pot-boilers ('Gaspar Ruiz', 'The Brute', 'An Anarchist' and 'The Informer'), and on parts of *The Mirror of the Sea*; he was also struggling with a novel – *Chance*. But, as had already happened in the case of *Lord Jim*, there came a sudden impulse to lay aside an overdue novel in order to start what was thought of as only a short story. For this is how Conrad described the thirteen pages that he sent to Pinker, under the title 'Verloc'.

In the event, though 'Verloc' was not destined to be a short story, it was written much more rapidly than *Chance*, if not quite as 'continuously' as Conrad later said in his 'Author's Note' to *The Secret Agent* (1920). In April the Conrads moved back from France to England, and it was in their farmhouse, The Pent, near Aldington in Kent, with brief stays in Ford Madox Ford's house in nearby Winchelsea, and in the Galsworthys' London house, that the first version of *The Secret Agent* was finished early in November 1906. By then *A Secret Agent* was already appearing in a new American magazine, *Ridgway's: A Militant Weekly for God and Country*, beginning on 6 October.

Before he had finished the serial version Conrad knew that he would have to do much more work before *The*

Secret Agent was ready for final publication in book form. This revision and expansion was begun that winter, with further work on the proofs from May to July of the next year. Here again Conrad was working under desperate pressure. Back in Montpellier, and later in Geneva, Conrad's eldest son Borys was twice very seriously ill; their newly born second son, John, almost died of whooping cough; while both Conrad himself and his wife Jessie were often in bad health. In addition, Conrad's financial affairs were more than usually threatening. He was working on *Chance* again, and on two short stories, 'Il Conde' and 'The Duel'; but it was on the popular success of *The Secret Agent* that he set his hopes of financial salvation, when it finally appeared in September 1907.

The primary document on the composition of *The Secret Agent* is the Author's Note which Conrad wrote in 1920 for the collected edition. Both in this preface, and in the letters which were written at the time of composition, Conrad was much more explicit than usual about his artistic and moral aims. For this reason most of these letters are reproduced below, and in sufficient detail to set Conrad's views of the novel in the context of his day-to-day domestic harassments.

Joseph Conrad to J. B. Pinker, Montpellier, 5 March 1906

My Dear Pinker,

Here's the text of the *Mirror of the Sea* ready at last. It is surprising how much time was taken up in putting it into some shape; but at any rate the proof corrections are not likely to go beyond the limit fixed by agreement. There will be no printers' bill for me to settle.

With the copy there is a loose leaf containing instructions which should be attended to.

I breathe a prayer for the book's success – the best success a book of that sort can reasonably expect. I'll put in motto and dedication in the first proof of title page, when I get it.

If you can spare me that fifty from the book advance you'll be working towards a happy release from worries. It isn't quite all that is necessary but it'll go a long way towards it. By and by when I've sent you a short story (to follow *Verloc*), there will be an amount of £16, another of about £20 and the income tax to pay. Meantime they must wait.

Verloc has been delayed rather by this *Mirror*. I sat up 3 nights. To have all my stuff in bits and scraps of print like this, confused my mind in a perfectly ridiculous manner. But it's over ! For all my efforts at economy I find the money goes quicker than I expected. The only luxury I have allowed myself is to get riding lessons for Borys. I have taken a series of twelve tickets which cost me 25/-. It's wonderful what good they are doing him; he looks a different child already; he was very white and peaked after his scarlet fever, with defective circulation too. Now all this is changed and I credit the horse with this improvement. As the father of a fine boy and a horseman yourself you'll understand my satisfaction at his shaping extremely well. From the very first day he had an excellent seat and a most amusing assurance on horseback. I daresay he inherits the instinct from his Polish ancestors. This week you'll get a further batch of *Verloc*. I don't like to say the final batch – but it's possible. Alas it'll be a longish story : 180,000 words or so, I fear. On the other hand, it is not a bad piece of work. We will see.[1]

During the summer of 1906 Conrad sent part of the manuscript of *The Secret Agent* to John Galsworthy. The terms of Conrad's thanks for Galsworthy's criticism in the ensuing letter must be read with the understanding that Galsworthy was considerably more sympathetic to radical movements and ideas than Conrad.

Joseph Conrad to John Galsworthy, 12 September 1906

Dearest Jack,

I've got the MS. this morning and before tackling the task of the day I want to thank you for your dear and good letter.

I am no end glad you like the thing generally.

The point of treatment you raise I have already considered. In such a tale one is likely to be misunderstood. After all, you must not take it too seriously. The whole thing is superficial and it is but a tale. I had no idea to consider Anarchism politically, or to treat it seriously in its philosophical aspect; as a manifestation of human nature in its discontent and imbecility. The general reflections whether right or wrong are not meant as bolts. You can't say I hurl them in any sense. They come in by the way and are not applicable to particular instances, – Russian or Latin. They are, if anything, mere digs at the people in the tale. As to attacking Anarchism as a form of humanitarian enthusiasm or intellectual despair or social atheism, that – if it were worth doing – would be the work for a more vigorous hand and for a mind more robust, and perhaps more honest than mine.

The diffuseness, pp. 141 to 151, depending on the state of the writer's health, has been felt, and shall be remedied in the measure of possibility.

As to the beastly trick of style, I have fallen into it through worry and hurry. I abominate it myself. It isn't even French really. It is Zola jargon simply. Why it should have fastened on me I don't know. But anything may happen to a man writing in a state of distraction. We shall see to that with great care when the tale is finished. You'll get a few pages more when Pinker returns them to me. The end is not yet, tho' 45 thousand words *are*.

And was Ada *really* interested?

Our dearest love to you both.[2]

Meanwhile Conrad was preparing the manuscript for book publication with Methuen's. Algernon Methuen requested material for a blurb, and provoked a typically haughty reply :

Joseph Conrad to Algernon Methuen, 7 November 1906

Dear Mr Methuen,

Thanks for your letter with enclosures. I quite understand the object of a descriptive note in a catalogue or circular. I have some notion too of the methods of publishing. I am acquainted with one of the best travellers in the trade. And as to the 'notes' in question, poor W. H. Chesson used to write them very skilfully for T. F. Unwin's publications – my own early novels amongst others. I have also a pretty clear idea who wrote these 'notes' for Mr Heinemann and for Messrs Blackwood. The point is that I was never asked to furnish that sort of thing myself. And I still think that the author is not the proper person for that work.

I've a very definite idea of what I tried to do and a fairly correct one (I hope) of what I *have* done. But it isn't a matter for a bookseller's ear. I don't think he would understand : I don't think many readers will. But that's not my affair. A piece of literary work may be defined in twenty ways. The people who are serializing the *Secret Agent* in the U.S. now have found their own definition. They described it (on posters) as 'A Tale of Diplomatic Intrigue and Anarchist Treachery'. But they don't do it on my authority and that's all I care for.

I could never have found that. I confess that in my eyes the story is a fairly successful (and sincere) piece of ironic treatment applied to a special subject – a sensational subject if one likes to call it so. And it is based on the inside knowledge of a certain event in the history of active anarchism. But otherwise it is *purely a work of imagination.* It has no social or philosophical intention. It is, I humbly

hope, not devoid of artistic value. It may have some moral
significance. It is also Conrad's writing. I should not be
surprised if it were violently attacked. And when it is prepared for 'book form' it will be 68,000 words in length –
or perhaps even more.

In this connection I wanted to ask you whether it would
be possible to have the book set up and *galley slips* pulled
off for me to work on? I would like it done very much unless
the cost of such self-indulgence were ruinous. I would send
the type-script at once to you. . . .[3]

On 13 March Conrad wrote to Pinker that in order to
complete *Chance* (which actually appeared only in 1913)
he didn't want to see the galleys of *The Secret Agent* until
June. The unexpected arrival of page proofs in May
created disgusted consternation :

Joseph Conrad to J. B. Pinker, 18 May 1907

My Dear Pinker,

Thank you very much for the money sent. If I telegraphed
on the 14th, it was because our rooms were let already and
had to be vacated. Moreover, I had a compartment reserved
in the train for the 15th. I have miscalculated my expenses
in Montpellier and must ask you to send frcs. 1100 by means
of Crédit Lyonnais to *Mr Joseph Ducailler*, Riche Hôtel,
Montpellier, in the course of the week. I left that much in
his debt. And please don't scold me, because I have just
now as much as I can bear. Here I am stranded again with
baby at its last gasp with whooping cough. It began in
Montpellier. We started by medical advice, counting on
the change of climate to check the disease, but it has developed on the road in a most alarming manner. The poor
little devil has melted down to half his size. Since yesterday
morning he has had a coughing fit every quarter of an hour
or so and will not eat anything. We'll have to resort to arti-

ficial feeding very soon. Of course *la Roseraie Hotel* [near Geneva] won't take us now. We stick here isolated at the end of a corridor. Really I haven't got my share of the commonest sort of luck. I suppose *Chance* will have to pay for all this. But if you think I ought to come home I will do so as soon as baby can travel, and will let my cure go to the devil. Borys of course has whooping cough too, but very mildly. Still, it isn't good for him. My dear Pinker, I feel that all this is almost too much for me.

I am trying to keep a steady mind and not allow myself to dwell too much on the cost of things or I would go distracted.

The proofs of *S.[ecret] A.[gent]* have reached me, and I have almost cried at the sight. I thought it was arranged beyond doubt that I was to have *galley slips* for my corrections. Instead of that, I get the proofs of set pages! Apart from the cost of corrections, which will be greatly augmented through that, there is the material difficulty of correcting clearly and easily on small margins. And upon my word, I don't want just now any extra difficulties put in the way of my work. I am hurt at Methuen disregarding my perfectly reasonable wishes in such a manner. If Alston Rivers can always furnish galley proofs to Hueffer, Methuen could well do that much for me. I feel their carelessness in this matter as a slight. Please tell them on the telephone from me that I have no photograph to send them. They bother me for that.

In the circumstances, after reflecting on the best way of dealing with the *S. A.*, I think I *must* curtail my corrections as much as possible. I have begun to correct and shall be sending you the first signatures as I finish them off. Meantime I shall lay *Chance* aside entirely – either the writing or the copying. The delay won't be long. Don't let your editor in the States slip away. Promise him a big lot of stuff by September. You can do that safely.

The *S. A.* approached with a fresh eye does not strike me as bad at all. There is an element of popularity in it. By this I don't mean to say that the thing is likely to be popular. I merely think that it shows traces of capacity for that sort of treatment which may make a novel popular.

As I've told you my mind runs much on popularity now. I would try to reach it not by sensationalism but by means of taking a widely discussed subject for the *text* of my novel. Apart from religious problems the public mind runs on questions of war and peace and labour. I mean war, peace, labour in general, not any particular form of labour trouble.

My head is in such a state that I don't know whether I make my idea clear. In short, my idea is to treat those subjects in a novel with a sufficiently interesting story, whose notion has come into my head lately. And of course to treat them from a modern point of view. All this is vague enough to talk about, but the plan in my mind is fairly definite. I will hurry on with that directly I've done with *Chance*. There is no time to lose.

Please drop me a line on receipt of this. I feel most awfully lonely and am putting all my trust in you to see me through.[4]

The following extracts from three letters written from Geneva to John Galsworthy continue the agonising story of the preparation of *The Secret Agent* for the press:

Joseph Conrad to John Galsworthy, 6 June 1907

Dear Jack,

Borys is very plucky with the pain. I believe he cried a little to his mother once, but never before me who am his principal attendant. It's I who break into a cold sweat when I hear a beastly fit of whooping cough shaking him all over, – with his four rheumatic joints. However there are only three now : both wrists and one elbow. He has no more pain in his feet, but they are no use whatever as yet. This has been going on for a fortnight nearly : the temperature from 100° to 101°. He hasn't lost his pluck, but he's losing his spring and lies very quiet and resigned, all eyes

as to his face and skin and bones as to the body. I read to
him all day and attend to him the best I can with one arm,
because my left, since my last gout, isn't much use : and
what I can do with it is done at the cost of a good deal of
pain. Now and then I steal an hour or two to work at preparing the *Secret Agent* for book form. And all this is
ghastly. I seem to move, talk, write in a sort of quiet nightmare that goes on and on. I wouldn't wish my worst enemy
this experience.

Poor little Jack has melted down to nothing in our hands.
He, however, seems to have turned the corner. But all his
little ribs can be seen at a glance. To-day he smiled distinctly the first time in the last 30 days or so, and with a
pathetically skinny little paw reached for my nose nippers.
I mention these favourable symptoms lest you should think
this letter unduly pessimistic.

From the sound next door (we have three rooms) I know
that the pain has roused Borys from his feverish doze. I
won't go to him. It's no use. Presently I shall give him his
salicylate, take his temperature and shall then go to elaborate a little more the conversation of Mr Verloc with his
wife. It is very important that the conversation of Mr
Verloc with his wife should be elaborated, – made more
effective, don't you know, – more *true* to the situation and
the character of these people.

By Jove ! I've got to hold myself with both hands not to
burst into a laugh which would scare wife, baby and the
other invalid, – let alone the lady whose room is on the other
side of the corridor ! . . .[5]

Joseph Conrad to John Galsworthy, 17 June 1907

Dearest Jack,
Borys does not get on at all. Symptoms of bronchitis at
the top of left lung have declared themselves since the 15th,
and there is the pleurisy too. With this a hectic fever well

characterized and rapid emaciation with a cough. It is his 22nd day in bed. Things could not look much more ugly. Another doctor is coming this afternoon.

I am keeping up, but I feel as if a mosquito bite were enough to knock me over. Good God! If I were to get it now, what would happen! As it is I don't know very well what will happen. It will be nothing good anyway, – even at best. And how to face it mentally and materially is what keeps my nerves on the stretch.

I thought I had told you I was setting the *Secret Agent* for book form. There was an additional chapter to write. That's done. Two chapters to expand – which I am now trying to do. Impossibility to get away from here. Dread of going back to the Pent : a sort of feeling that this is the end of things at the end of twelve years' work, – all this does not help me much in making Mr & Mrs Verloc effective for the amusement of a public, – which won't be amused by me at all. . . .[6]

Joseph Conrad to John Galsworthy, 30 July 1907

Dear Jack,

At last I can tell you that Borys's convalescence may be considered as ended. The period of picking up strength has begun. We had various alarms, but that seems all over now. It has been altogether a ghastly time, – from the 15th May to the 15th July. In that time I've written roughly speaking 28 to 30,000 words in order to make a decent book of the *Secret Agent*.

I think it's pretty good – for what it is. The pages you've marked for cancellation (or cancelling?) in the typescript are retained after a proper amount of thinking over. They fall in pretty well with the ironic scheme of the book, – and the public can skip if it likes.

We return soon. My health is comparatively good, but my anxieties have been increased by all that happened in the last four or rather five months. We shall try to pick up the old existence, somewhat nearer London than the Pent. But everything is difficult in my position. I look forward with dread to an effort which, I fear, from the nature of things, can never any more be adequate.

It shall be made of course, but the feeling is against the probability of success. Art, truth, expression are difficult enough by themselves, – God knows ! . . .[7]

On the same day as this letter Conrad also wrote an important estimate of *The Secret Agent* to Pinker:

Joseph Conrad to J. B. Pinker, 30 July 1907

My Dear Pinker,

Thanks for the money. The book I think is a book to produce some sensation. I don't say it is good, but I say it is the best I could do with the subject. In the months of the boy's illness I managed to write into it some 26–28,000 words. After that I imagine I can do anything; for you can have no idea of my mental state all that time. Besides the anxiety for the child, there was the tearing awful worry of the circumstances.

After getting back to the Pent the great thing will be to get away from there as soon as possible, and make a fresh start.

There will be the house hunting. Perhaps we may get something near Ashford to make the moving less expensive. If you hear of any inexpensive sort of house in the country near London make a note of it for us.

I reckon 4 months for *Chance* counting from 1st of August, for I am not going house hunting as you may imagine. At the Pent I will go to work. But it is of the utmost importance for me to get settled for good. Moreover the Pent is damnably expensive to live in. The idea is to have no bills. One spends always more than one intends to do. But all this will not be possible till we've got clear of the place.

I think I can say safely that the *Secret Agent* is not the sort of novel to make what comes after more difficult to place. Neither will it, I fancy, knock my prices down. *Chance* itself will be altogether different in tone and treatment of course, but it will be salable I believe. By the end of Sept^er you will have a really considerable lot of it to show. Of course it will not be on popular lines. Nothing of mine can be, I fear. But even Meredith ended by getting his sales. Now, I haven't Meredith's delicacy, and that's a point in my favour. I reckon I may make certain of the support of the Press for the next few years. The young men who are coming in to write criticisms are in my favour so far. At least all of whom I've heard are. I don't get in the way of established reputations. One may read everybody and yet in the end want to read me – for a change if for nothing else. For I don't resemble anybody; and yet I am not specialized enough to call up imitators as to matter or style. There is nothing in me but a turn of mind which, whether valuable or worthless, cannot be imitated.

It has been a disastrous time. You must help me settle down now on an economical basis. It will cost something to do that but, that once done, 3 years of close sitting will do the trick. I'll be then 52 and not worn out yet as a writer. Without exaggeration I may say I feel renovated by my cure here – and considering the adverse circumstances, this seems a good sign. I am anxious to get back and drive on.

We could start from here on the 10th. I would like to start on that date. I would go on the 8th, providing always you pay the people in Kent before I return in accordance with the enclosed list. . . . No more trips abroad. I am sick of them.[8]

NOTES

1. Conrad's detailed explanation of Borys's riding lessons must be read in the context of the fact that Pinker, the greatest and in many ways the most generous of literary agents of

the day, had made very large advances to Conrad since their association began in 1901; at this time Conrad owed Pinker well over £1,000. (The letter is quoted from G. Jean-Aubry, *Joseph Conrad: Life and Letters* (London : Heinemann, 1927) II 30–1. This and later letters by Joseph Conrad are reproduced by permission of the Trustees of the Joseph Conrad Estate.)

2. The two men had been friends since 1892 when Galsworthy was a passenger from Adelaide to England on the *Torrens*, a sailing ship of which Conrad was first mate. Ada is Galsworthy's wife. (Jean-Aubry, *Life and Letters*, II 32–3.)

3. Conrad's estimate of the final length of *The Secret Agent* was some 40,000 words short of the eventual 105,000 words, though closer than his earlier estimate of 180,000 in the letter to Pinker above. (Jean-Aubry, *Life and Letters*, II 38–9.)

4. Ibid. 48–9.

5. Ibid. 51–2.

6. Ibid. 52–3.

7. Ibid. 53–4.

8. Ibid. 54–5. *Chance* was only finished in 1912.

The *Secret Agent* was published in September 1907 both
in London and New York. The story of its mixed reception is told in the following selection of letters and contemporary reviews.

In England *The Secret Agent* was published by
Methuen at the then normal price of 6s. On 20 Septem-
ber 1907 Conrad sent a copy to his 'Très Cher Maître',
Henry James, with the laconic comment :

I am sending you my latest volume. Receive it with the
indulgence which cannot be refused to a profound and
sincere sentiment prompting the act. The covers are deep
red I believe. As to what's inside of them I assure you I
haven't the slightest idea. That's where Hazlitt's Indian
Juggler has the pull over a writer of tales. He at least knows
how many balls he is keeping up in the air at the same
time. . . .[1]

Conrad's letters of the next few weeks reflect the
'honourable failure' of *The Secret Agent* as regards reviews and sales. Thus a letter to Pinker written at the end
of September, though mentioning several private letters
of praise, reveals Conrad's anxiety about whether the
novel would have a second edition. The letter also refers
to an extremely hostile review in *Country Life* :

Joseph Conrad to J. B. Pinker, 27(?) September 1907

My Dear Pinker,
Thanks for your letter ever so much. I was not unduly
impressed by the *Country Life* slating. I could write a jolly

sight better slating myself of that book – something that
would get home on to its defects. . . .

Talking of effect. Is the *S[ecret]* *A[gent]* producing any
on the public? I wish I knew, mainly for this reason, that if
there's going to be a second edition soon (or at all) I would
like to correct a few horrid misprints there are – if that can
be done.

Graves wrote me a nice letter a day or two ago. Who is
the Buchan you mention in yours? Is he John Buchan who
used to write in *Blackwood's* 3 years ago? Graves is a good
friend to have – apart from being a sympathetic person to
know. [E. V.] Lucas wrote to me too with enthusiasm.
A. J. Dawson also – only yesterday. But from Edward
Garnett I haven't heard privately, tho' I know he is to review the book somewhere.[2]

The anonymous review referred to was as follows:

Country Life, 21 September 1907: A Book of the Week

Until *The Secret Agent* (Methuen) came into my hands
my ideas of Mr Joseph Conrad were of the vaguest. Some
years ago I looked into a book, a novel of sea life, written
by him, and formed a high opinion of his potentialities.
Since then rumour has been busy with his name, and
he is now almost invariably spoken of in respectful terms
as a writer of very great ability, who has a magnificent
future before him. Possibly this may be quite true, but
the augury is not borne out by the latest of his publications. *The Secret Agent*, subjected to any test that can be
imagined, will not entitle the author to a place beside
Scott and Thackeray. One would begin by saying something about his selection of characters, although it may
be said that the first, second, third and last essential is
that they should be interesting. Unless the creations of
an author's brain seize the attention and exercise the mind

of his readers they are not worth considering at all; but a less amusing set of people never filled the imaginary world of a novelist than have been chosen for the pages of *The Secret Agent*. There used to be an old song of which the refrain, if we remember rightly, was: 'It's naughty, but it's nice.' Now, Mr Conrad, in this book, is naughty, without being at all nice. His chief male character is a Mr Verloc, a sort of spy and informer in the service of revolutionists. In portraying him the author appears to have taken M. Zola as model, for he introduces him with a certain kind of respectability, making him decent in his indecency, and honest in his dishonesty. The thing strikes us at once as a paradox. The sort of shop kept by Mr Verloc is one where shady photographs, obscene literature and other articles of a similar kind are sold. The people who keep such places are, generally speaking, the most unmitigated blackguards who hold on to the edges of civilisation. The man, however, as depicted by Mr Conrad might have been an honest plasterer or stonemason, who has even gone on the path of respectability so far as to get married, instead of forming one of the slight and fleeting attachments which are more common in the order to which he belongs. His wife – and thereby hangs a tale – is the daughter of a woman who has kept a boarding-house and is the widow of a low type of licensed victualler or publican. The man is a very dull dog who, apparently, has a gift for spouting in parks and places where Socialists assemble, but shows very little trace indeed of eloquence in the conversations he holds with the various people during the course of this story. Indeed, it would appear as if Mr Conrad had set himself the impossible task of trying to make dulness interesting, for he lets Verloc only use a hoarse whisper in private, instead of a voice that was said to carry over the greater extent of Hyde Park; and he is distinguished,

more than in any other way, by an utter lack of wit and
esprit. He is called upon by an ambassador to destroy one
of the great scientific institutions in Great Britain.

I would never dream of directing you to organise a mere
butchery, even if I expected the best results from it. But I
wouldn't expect from a butchery the result I want. Murder is always with us. It is almost an institution. The demonstration must be against learning – science. But not every
science will do. The attack must have all the shocking sense-
lessness of gratuitous blasphemy. Since bombs are your
means of expression, it would be really telling if one could
throw a bomb into pure mathematics. But that is impossible.

This reminds us curiously of one of Mr Gilbert's phan-
tasies, only it is a Gilbertian idea clothed in very bad
prose. The respectable vendor of photographs is, to use a
colloquialism, 'knocked silly' by this demand upon his
energies, and yet he has to set about carrying out the
command laid upon him with diligence, lest those of his
own brotherhood should fall upon and slay him. The
brotherhood consists of a number of very stagey revolutionists. One of them is a little man, who goes about
armed with a new detonator, with which he is prepared
to blow himself into eternity when any attempt is made
to arrest him. He, too, might have figured quite appro-
priately in Gilbert and Sullivan's opera; but all this is
not germane to Mr Conrad's intention, which is obviously to develop the latent capacity for murder in Mrs
Verloc. She has married this agent without any question
of love coming in the way, but merely because she had
two people to provide for – her mother and a half-witted
brother. Jilted by a butcher boy, in the days when she
was serving-maid at the boarding-house, all that she has
of love and passion has flowed out to this half-witted
brother. Him Mr Verloc chooses as the agent to carry

out his plan of destroying the Hall of Science. The youth
fails to do it, and is blown into so many pieces that – as
our author tells us with a realism that seems to have tickled
his palate – they have to be collected in two shovels.
About half-a-dozen times these implements and their
grim contents are referred to in the story. This catastrophe
enrages Mrs Verloc, who stabs her husband and afterwards commits suicide. That is the sum and substance of
the story. If Mrs Verloc had been interesting, the tale
would have been so as well; but, if possible, she is still
duller than her husband. This fact is emphasised by the
very bad style in which Mr Conrad tells his story. You
can tell a great writer at once, because his analysis is all
done, as it were, behind the curtain. He makes his people
speak and act, and leaves the reader to judge what is
passing in their minds. The course followed by Mr Conrad is exactly the opposite of this. In page after page he
discourses fluently about the ideas that were coursing
through the brain of a woman who never spoke at all.
The sort of writing we refer to may be shown by a speci-
men :

Every nook and cranny of her brain was filled with the
thought that this man, with whom she had lived without
distaste for seven years, had taken the 'poor boy' away from
her in order to kill him – the man to whom she had grown
accustomed in body and mind; the man whom she had
trusted, took the boy away to kill him! In its form, in its
substance, in its effect, which was universal, altering even
the aspect of inanimate things, it was a thought to sit still
at and marvel at for ever and ever. Mrs Verloc sat still.
And across that thought (not across the kitchen) the form
of Mr Verloc went to and fro, familiarly in hat and overcoat, stamping with his boots upon her brain. He was probably talking too; but Mrs Verloc's thought for the most
part covered the voice.

But when we tell the reader that this sort of thing goes on for seventy-five pages – to be exact, from page 301 to 376 – he will see what we mean. Of course, the art that perpetrates this sort of thing is very bad indeed. Nothing can be called art except that which is convincing, and the reader knows absolutely that Mr Conrad is guessing, and guessing very badly, at the intricate movements of a woman's mind. There is no way by means of which he could get within it. Indeed, we had thought that the style of writing here exemplified belonged to an earlier and less enlightened stage in our literary history. It places Mr Conrad not in the van, where he ought to be, but in the rear of the movement. Again, we have no hesitation in saying that the whole thing is indecent. Of course, we do not apply the term in the vulgar meaning; what we call indecent is that the whole inception, process and accomplishment of a murder should have been planned, as it were, on the stage and in the sight of the spectators. Killing, undoubtedly, is a necessity; but it is as indecent to exhibit a murder done in this slow and tedious manner as it would be to have the shambles of a butcher in the public streets. Many chapters before it takes place we know perfectly well what is coming. The art that conceals art is not Mr Conrad's; but this is not all the fault we have to find with *The Secret Agent*. Critics generally have agreed that even very great authors, such as Fielding, made a mistake in keeping to the example of Cervantes, and introducing short stories into the middle of their novels. Mr Conrad is not guilty of that mistake, but of one equally inartistic, and that is the fault of bringing in minor and unessential characters and making far too much of them. It is best to give specific examples, so that any reader can, if he wishes, turn up the book and see for himself, or herself, how far these strictures are justified. Let us take chap. viii as an example. It tells us

how Mrs Verloc's mother went about to get admitted
to an almshouse. The incident in itself is well enough, and
might be helpful in developing the character of Mrs
Verloc; but considering that the woman never comes
into the story again, the enormously-drawn-out tale of
her departure must be considered as an excrescence, was
not wanted in the slightest. Again, the characters of the
Assistant Commissioner, the Inspector of Police, and the
Minister, whose portrait seems to be intended as a burlesque of the late Sir William Harcourt, are all unneces-
sary to the picture, and might have been left out, or their
parts curtailed, to very great advantage. In fact, if Mr
Conrad was aiming at art and immortality instead of at
filling up a definite number of pages, he could have reduced this story to a tenth part of its present dimensions,
and still rather added to than taken away from its merits.
The book might fairly be described as a study of murder,
by a writer with a personality as egotistical as that of Mr
Bernard Shaw, only lacking in the wit and humour which
goes some way to justify the existence of the latter.   Z.

*

Such complacency of patronage was no doubt to be expected from *Country Life*, although even so to accuse
Conrad of belonging to 'an earlier and less enlightened
stage in our literary history' seems as grotesque an irony
as any in *The Secret Agent*. It may also be noted that
Country Life's sympathy with the *avant-garde* did not
extend to its social views. In his next review of a novel,
Maurice Hewlett's *The Stooping Lady*, we find 'Z'
roundly declaring : 'The very theme is slightly displeas-
ing. . . . It is a tale of a woman of the patrician class, who
fell in love with a butcher.'

Most of the other English reviews of *The Secret Agent* were more respectful, although the note of disappointment was rarely absent. One notable exception to this was the *Times Literary Supplement* :

Times Literary Supplement, 20 September 1907

Mr Joseph Conrad, by a stroke of fine humour, has appended to his new book, *The Secret Agent* (Methuen, 6s.), a history of anarchists and spies, the sub-title 'A Simple Tale'; and in thinking it over we have suddenly realized that a part at least of this great novelist's mission is to remind his readers how simple men really are, even when they are the destroyers of society or their pursuers. To show how narrow a gulf is fixed between the maker of bombs and the ordinary contented citizen has never before struck a novelist as worth while, the subterranean world in which the terrorists live having up to the present time been considered by him merely as a background for lurid scenes and hair-raising thrills. And then comes Mr Conrad with his steady, discerning gaze, his passion for humanity, his friendly irony, and above all his delicate and perfectly tactful art, to make them human and incidentally to demonstrate how monotonous a life can theirs also be. Stevenson just dipped into this nether world, bringing away only what was needed for his more or less sensational purpose; it was left for Mr Conrad once again to hold the lantern that was to light every cranny; just as it was left for him fully to illumine the darkest places of the forecastle, the swamps of the Congo, and the mysteries of the heart of the revolutionary, the Ishmael, the derelict, and the coward. Englishmen cannot be too grateful that this alien of genius, casting about for a medium in which to express his sympathy and his knowledge, hit upon our own tongue. *The Secret Agent* is more of a portrait gallery than a story, although it is a story too, and a really exciting one. It is notable, we think, chiefly for the portrait of the Professor the maker of bombs, Mr Verloc the spy, and Chief Inspector Heat, of Scotland-yard, hunter of men; but there is no one scamped in it; all are made vivid, and their interaction is marvellously managed. The logic of the story is of iron. We do not consider *The Secret Agent* Mr Conrad's masterpiece; it lacks the free movement of *Youth* and the terrible minuteness of *Lord Jim*, while it offers no scope for the employment of the tender and warm fancy that made *Karain* so memorable; but it is, we think, an advance upon *Nostromo*, its immediate predecessor. That canvas was a little overcrowded, while in *The Secret Agent* one's way is clear throughout. But the Professor is its triumph. It is the Professor who principally increases Mr Conrad's reputation, already of the highest.

*

The *Spectator* also was highly laudatory :

Spectator, 21 September 1907

THE SECRET AGENT

Mr Joseph Conrad on the few occasions hitherto when he has laid his scene in England has failed to exert the sombre fascination which marks his pictures of the unchanging East and the changeless ocean. There is something about his genius that ill accords with the amenities and actualities of a normal humdrum home-keeping existence. But

London is a microcosm, a *colluvies gentium*, and there are phases and aspects of London life mysterious and unfamiliar enough to appeal to his exotic imagination. It was a sure instinct that guided him in the present instance to choose for his *milieu* the colony of Anarchists and revolutionists who find asylum in our midst, and the result is a psychological romance of terrorism at once so subtle and yet so engrossing as to maintain, and even advance, his reputation as a literary sorcerer of the first rank.

When Mr Conrad calls his story a 'simple tale' he is perhaps overestimating the intelligence of the average reader. But allowing for his occasional disregard of chronological order, and for certain characteristic perversities of method, the main motive of the book is clear enough, and the narrative tolerably easy to follow. The central figure is a Mr Verloc, a man of uncertain foreign extraction and dubious antecedents, who has for many years been settled in London, and employed as a salaried spy by a foreign Embassy. He is known to, and unofficially recognised by, the detective police, who in return for his information overlook the illicit character of the trade in which he is engaged; and, on the other hand, he has contrived to retain the confidence of the colony of Anarchists and revolutionaries who use his shop as a house of call. He is married to an English wife, and provides quarters for her invalid mother and half-witted brother. On his domestic, as opposed to his professional, side Mr Verloc is a humane and kindly man. But at the opening of the story his position is suddenly imperilled by the altered attitude of his principal employers. The old Ambassador, an extremely timid man with a high opinion of Verloc's abilities, has been replaced, and the new régime are dissatisfied with negative results and mere warnings. Mr Verloc is accordingly summoned to the Embassy and informed in so many words that his salary will cease unless he can stimulate the British Government to adopt sterner measures against Anarchist refugees. In other words, he is bidden to justify his existence by fulfilling the function of the *agent-provocateur* in its crudest form, – that of organising bogus outrages. More than that, M. Vladimir – who is the real villain of the plot – throws out a fantastic suggestion as to the lines on which the outrage might be carried out. It is with the effects of this suggestion on an essentially stupid man, panic-stricken by the prospect of ruin, and with the means of literally carrying out this wild hint placed at his disposal, that the tragic and terrible sequel is concerned. But while the secret agent is in a sense the central figure, he is less interesting and less convincing than many other personages, mostly sinister, whose portraits are drawn in these intricate, yet absorbing, pages. There are the group of Anarchists, mainly dominated by vanity, – the visionary Michaelis, the venomous Karl Yundt, Comrade Ossipon, bilker of confiding servant-girls, and, above all, the little Professor, the really dangerous, because absolutely fearless, apostle of destruction, whose sudden meeting with the Inspector after the bomb outrage is perhaps the most striking scene in the book. Then we have the noble patroness of Michaelis, the incarnation of detached curiosity; Chief Inspector Heat, able and efficient, but 'thinking of his superiors, of his reputation, of the Law Courts, of his salary, of newspapers'; his official chief, the Assistant-Commissioner, a man of real detective genius, but hampered by departmental conventions and personal obligations. And as a background to this sombre drama of the conflict between the conservators and the enemies of the social system there is London in its immensity and mystery, enveloped in the strange atmosphere diffused by the sardonic genius of Mr Conrad.

Mr Conrad's knowledge and appreciation of London

– not only the subterranean London of the refugee – is as remarkable as his penetrating insight into the psychology of the monstrous brood of enigmatical persons which it harbours. Take, for example, the passage in which he describes Mr Verloc's progress to the Embassy on the occasion of his eventful visit :

Before reaching Knightsbridge, Mr Verloc took a turn to the left out of the busy main thoroughfare, uproarious with the traffic of swaying omnibuses and trotting vans, in the almost silent, swift flow of hansoms. Under his hat, worn with a slight backward tilt, his hair has been carefully brushed into respectful sleekness; for his business was with an Embassy. And Mr Verloc, steady like a rock – a soft kind of rock – marched now along a street which could with every propriety be described as private. In its breadth, emptiness, and extent it had the majesty of inorganic nature, of matter that never dies. The only reminder of mortality was a doctor's brougham arrested in august solitude close to the curbstone. The polished knockers of the doors gleamed as far as the eye could reach, the clean windows shone with a dark opaque lustre. And all was still. But a milk cart rattled noisily across the distant perspective; a butcher boy, driving with the noble recklessness of a charioteer at Olympic Games, dashed round the corner sitting high above a pair of red wheels. A guilty-looking cat issuing from under the stones ran for a while in front of Mr Verloc, then dived into another basement; and a thick police constable, looking a stranger to every emotion, as if he too were part of inorganic nature, surging apparently out of a lamp-post, took not the slightest notice of Mr Verloc. With a turn to the left Mr Verloc pursued his way along a narrow street by the side of a yellow wall which, for some inscrutable reason, had No. 1 Chesham Square written on it in black letters. Chesham Square was at least sixty yards away, and Mr Verloc, cosmopolitan enough not to be deceived by London's topographical mysteries, held on steadily, without a sign of surprise or indignation. At last with business-like persistency, he reached the Square, and made diagonally for the number 10. This belonged to an imposing carriage gate in a high, clean wall between two houses, of which one rationally enough bore the number 9 and the other was numbered 37; but the fact that this last belonged to Porthill Street, a street well known in the neighbourhood, was proclaimed by an inscription placed above the ground-floor windows by whatever highly efficient authority is charged with the duty of keeping track of London's strayed houses. Why powers are not asked of Parliament (a short act would do) for compelling those edifices to return where they belong is one of the mysteries of municipal administration.

In another vein, and as illustrating Mr Conrad's gift for richly suggestive characterisation, we may quote his striking picture of the lady patroness of Michaelis, 'the ticket-of-leave apostle of humanitarian hopes' :

Married young and splendidly at some remote epoch of the past, she had had for a time a close view of great affairs and even of some great men. She herself was a great lady. Old now in the number of her years, she had that sort of exceptional temperament which defies time with scornful disregard, as if it were a rather vulgar convention submitted to by the mass of inferior mankind. Many other conventions easier to set aside, alas! failed to obtain her recognition, also on temperamental grounds – either because they bored her, or else because they stood in the way of her scorns and sympathies. Admiration was a sentiment unknown to her (it was one of the secret griefs of her most noble husband against her) – first, as. always more or less tainted with mediocrity, and next as being in a way an admission of inferiority. And both were frankly inconceivable to her nature. To be fearlessly outspoken in her opinions came easily to her, since she judged solely from the standpoint of her social position. She was equally untrammelled in her actions; and as her tactfulness proceeded from genuine humanity, her bodily vigour remained remarkable and her superiority was serene and cordial, three generations had admired her infinitely, and the last she was likely to see had pronounced her a wonderful woman. Meantime intelligent, with a sort of lofty simplicity, and curious at heart, but not like many women merely of social gossip, she amused her age by attracting within her ken through the power of her great, almost historical, social prestige everything that rose above the dead level of mankind, lawfully or unlawfully, by position, wit, audacity, fortune or misfortune. Royal Highnesses, artists, men of science, young statesmen, and charlatans of all ages and conditions, who, unsubstantial and light, bobbing up like corks, show best the direction of the surface currents, had been welcomed in that house, listened to, penetrated, understood, appraised, for her own edification. In her own words, she liked to watch what the world was coming to. And as she had a practical mind her judgment of men and things, though based on special prejudices, was seldom totally wrong, and almost never wrong-headed. Her drawing-room was probably the only place in the wide world where an Assistant Commissioner of Police could meet a convict liberated on a ticket-of-leave on other than professional and official ground.

There are certain obvious blemishes in this book. There is a murder which we cannot regard as justifiable either by logic or art. There is inconsistency in the development of the character of Mr Verloc, and grave improbability in the immunity from police interference so long enjoyed by the Professor. There are digressions, admirable in themselves, which interrupt the march of the narrative in a tantalising manner. Fastidious readers, again, may be repelled by certain gruesome details given in the pages describing the results of the explosion. But, to speak truly,

such criticism, though legitimate, is largely disarmed in
presence of a work so rich in surprise and suspense, so
original in conception and treatment, – so lavishly endowed, in fine, with the singular qualities which have
won for Mr Conrad a unique position amongst the British
novelists of to-day.

*

The most interesting review for us, as no doubt for Conrad, was Edward Garnett's column on 'The Novel of the
Week' in *The Nation* :

The Nation, 28 September 1907

It is good for us English to have Mr Conrad in our midst
visualising for us aspects of life we are constitutionally
unable to perceive, for by his astonishing mastery of our
tongue he makes clear to his English audience those secrets
of Slav thought and feeling which seem so strange and in-
accessible in their native language. They are not inacces-
sible, those secrets, not in the least; through the gates of
literary translations we can all enter into the alien spirit
of those distant peoples; but so poor is the imagination
of most of us that we linger outside, puzzled and repelled
by their strange atmosphere and environment, even when
mirrored clearly by art. Mr Conrad, however, is to us as
a willing hostage we have taken from the Slav lands, in
exchange for whom no ransom could outweigh the value
of his insight and his artistic revelation of the world at
our gates, by us so imperfectly apprehended. By *The
Secret Agent* he has added to the score of our indebtedness, and he has brought clearly into our ken the sub-

terranean world of that foreign London which, since the death of Count Fosco, has served in fiction only the crude purpose of our sensational writers.

The Secret Agent opens with an amazingly clever interview between the two bureaucrats of a foreign embassy, M. Vladimir and Privy Councillor Wurmt, and one of their secret agents, or spies, Mr Verloc, who, French by origin, would probably have attained to affluence as a Belgian official 'administering' the Congo. But Mr Verloc's destiny has relegated him to the less glorious profession of keeping a shady shop in a dingy street in Soho, under cover of which he carries on his real business of *agent provocateur* to the Embassy in question. MM. Wurmt and Vladimir, however, are no more satisfied with their secret agent's activities than they are with 'the general leniency of the judicial procedure in England, and the utter absence of police repressive measures', which, in their view, 'are a scandal to Europe'. They are new brooms in the Embassy, *vice* Baron Stott-Wartenheim deceased, and they are of opinion that the psychological moment has arrived when a series of anarchist outrages, cleverly fomented by Mr Verloc, will scare the middle classes and the police into repressive legislation against the revolutionary world of political refugees, anarchists, &c. M. Vladimir's cynical satisfaction and quick-witted versatility, as he develops the scheme by which the vigilance of the London police is to be 'stimulated' by his unhappy secret agent, is admirably rendered, and though the average Englishman may murmur, like Judge Brack in *Hedda Gabler*, 'such things *don't* happen', we may guess that M. Vladimir is fresh from contact with the Petersburg secret police. Mr Verloc, threatened with dismissal from his post 'if nothing happens', is both startled and alarmed, and he retires sadly to think out how he can best organise 'the demonstration', by which

our backward England is to be brought into line with
the Continental bureaucracies. And having hit off with a
sure and uncanny dexterity the point of view, shall we
say, of the ordinary Russian official in high places, Mr
Conrad turns his attention next to the underground world
of anarchism, to the official anxieties of the London police
– represented by Chief Inspector Heat and his Chief, the
Assistant-Commissioner – and to the domestic relations of
Mr Verloc, his wife, Winnie, and soft-headed brother,
Stevie, which are violently wound up by the blowing
to bits of the last, the suicide of the second, and the murder of the first.

In tracing the outline of this appallingly futile tragedy
the reviewer may remark that Mr Conrad's possession
of a philosophy, impartial in its scrutiny of the forces of
human nature, is the secret of his power – we had almost
added, of his superiority to contemporary English novelists. The laws that govern human nature are often as
disconcerting to our self-esteem as they are chastening to
our spiritual egoism. And our English novelists, unlike
the Slav, are apt to work too assiduously on the side of
the angels, and hold, avowedly or in secret, an ethical
brief. But the advantage of keeping the earthly horizon
on a low plane is that there is more space around and
beyond, in the picture, for the background of those eternal
elements which both govern and dwarf man's petty endeavour. Mr Conrad's achievement in his novels and
tales of seamen's life in the Eastern seas, was, in fact, a
poet's achievement; he showed us the struggle of man's
passionate and wilful endeavour, cast against the background of nature's infinity and passionless purpose. And
in *The Secret Agent* Mr Conrad's ironical insight into
the natural facts of life, into those permanent animal
instincts which underlie our spiritual necessities and
aspirations, serves him admirably in place of the mysteri-

ous backgrounds of tropical seas and skies to which he has accustomed us. He goes down into the dim recesses of human motive, but though his background is only the murky gloom of old London's foggy streets and squares, the effect is none the less arresting. His character sketches of Michaelis, the ticket-of-leave apostle of anarchism, of Karl Yundt, the famous terrorist, the moribund veteran of dynamite wars, 'who has been a great actor in his time, on platforms, in secret assemblies, in private interviews', but who has never, strange to say, put his theories into practice; of Comrade Ossipon, who lives by exploiting the servant-girls whom his handsome face has seduced; and of the Professor, the dingy little man whose ferocious hatred of social injustice inspires him with a moral force that makes both his posturing comrades and the police shudder, acutely conscious, as they are, that he has both the will and the means to shatter a streetful of people to bits – these character sketches supply us with a working analysis of anarchism that is profoundly true, though the philosophical anarchism of certain creative minds is, of course, out of the range of the author's survey. And not less well done is the scrutiny of the official *morale* and personal incentives that govern the conduct of those guardians of social order, Chief Inspector Heat and the Assistant-Commissioner of Police. The two men, who have different ends in view, typify the daily conflict between Justice as a means and Justice as an end, which two are indeed rarely in harmony.

But Mr Conrad's superiority over nearly all contemporary English novelists is shown in his discriminating impartiality which, facing imperturbably all the conflicting impulses of human nature, refuses to be biassed in favour of one species of man rather than another. Chief Inspector Heat, the thief-taker and the guardian of social order, is no better a man than the inflexible avenger of social injustice, the Professor. The Deputy Commissioner of Police, though a fearless and fine individual, moves our admiration no more than does the child-like idealist, Michaelis, who has been kept in prison for fifteen years for a disinterested act of courage. Whether the spy, Mr Verloc, is more contemptible than the suave and rosy-gilled favourite of London drawing-rooms, M. Vladimir, is as difficult a point to decide as whether the latter is less despicable than the robust seducer of women, the cowardly Comrade Ossipon. And, by a refined stroke of irony, the innocent victim of anarchist propaganda and bureaucratic counter-mining is the unfortunate and weak-witted lad, Stevie, whose morbid dread of pain is exploited by the bewildered *agent provocateur*, Mr Verloc, in his effort to serve the designs of his Embassy, and preserve both his situation and his own skin. Finally, as an illustration of our author's serene impartiality, we may mention that the real heroine of the story is concealed in the trivial figure of Mr Verloc's mother-in-law, whose effacement of self for the sake of her son, Stevie, is the cause contributory to his own and her daughter's ruin. For Mr Verloc, growing desperate, sends the half-witted lad with an infernal machine to blow up Greenwich Observatory, and, Stevie perishing, Mr Verloc is attacked by his wife in a fit of frenzy and killed.

While the psychological analysis of the characters' motives is as full of acumen as is the author's philosophical penetration into life, it is right to add that Mr Verloc and his wife are less convincing in their actions than in their meditations. There is a hidden weakness in the springs of impulse of both these figures, and at certain moments they become automata. But such defects are few. Mr Conrad's art of suggesting the essence of an atmosphere and of a character in two or three pages has never been more strikingly illustrated than in *The Secret*

Agent. It has the profound and ruthless sincerity of the great Slav writers mingled with the haunting charm that reminds us so often of his compatriot Chopin.

*

Only a rooted Slavophil obsession, we may feel, could lead anyone to find in *The Secret Agent* anything remotely evocative of Chopin's 'haunting charm'. Still, Garnett's general analysis seems perceptive enough; and if we consider the novel in the context of Edwardian literature there is much to be said for locating 'the secret of Conrad's power' in his refusal 'to work too assiduously on the side of the angels' according to some 'ethical brief'.

Conrad responded to his old friend's review with his usual hyperbolic warmth, which need not persuade us that Conrad wholly accepted Garnett's diagnosis of his failure with the psychology of the Verlocs.

Joseph Conrad to Edward Garnett, 1 October 1907

Dearest Edward.

I only heard from Jack [Galsworthy] yesterday of your review in the Nation. I sent to the Railway Station today for the No.

It makes a fine reading for an author and no mistake. I am no end proud to see you've spotted my poor old woman. You've got a fiendishly penetrating eye for one's most secret intentions. She *is* the heroine. And you are appallingly quick in jumping upon a fellow. Yes O ! yes my dear Edward – that's what's the matter with the estimable Verloc and his wife : 'the hidden weakness in the springs of impulse'. I was so convinced that something was wrong there that to read your definition has been an immense relief

– great enough to be akin to joy. The defect is so profoundly temperamental that to this moment I can't tell *how* I went wrong. Of going wrong I was aware even at the time of writing – all the time. You may imagine what a horrible grind it was to keep on going with this suspicion at the back of the head.

You must preach to me a little when we meet – and even pray over me if you only will. Unless you think I am past praying for.

Sitting here alone with the glowing lamp in this silent, as yet strange house, I feel a great affection for you – and a great confidence in your judgement. Twelve years now – just a round dozen my dear – since I hear your voice in my ear as I put aside each written page. Yes. A great affection and an absolute confidence.[3]

As the autumn wore on, the gloomy outlines of the picture slowly filled in. Conrad could now count on being treated with the deference due to an important established author; but the critics rarely talked as if they knew why. Like Garnett, they could never forget that Conrad was a Slav, and tended to treat him primarily as a curiosity. As Conrad wrote in his next letter to Garnett: 'I've been so cried up of late as a sort of freak, an amazing bloody foreigner writing in English (every blessed review of *S. A.* had it so – even yours). . . .'[4]

As to the substance of *The Secret Agent*, the reviewers tended to concentrate on the very things which were most likely to discourage the ordinary reader. There was the gloom, the amount of analysis, and a good deal of objection to the difficulty of the time scheme. The relaxed irony of Conrad's subtitle – 'A Simple Tale' – apparently escaped the *Athenaeum*'s reviewer, for instance, who stoutly took up the cudgels on behalf of 'the good soul who sets out to read for the story alone' :

Athenaeum, 28 September 1907

That Mr Conrad should describe his latest book in a sub-title as 'a simple tale' is of itself evidence of the remark-able character of his mind. There is reason to believe that he applies this description to *The Secret Agent* in all good faith. Yet, as a fact, the book is far more than a simple one, even for the expert; while for the average reader of novels there is nothing simple about it. No good judge is likely to accuse Mr Conrad of intentional obscur-ity in any of his fine work; but his temperament and mind are remarkable and rare. The fact has enriched English fiction during the past decade to the extent of a dozen stories of singular merit. It also has carried a penalty, for Mr Conrad. The subtlety of his mental processes, the keenness of his artistic senses, have placed him further away from the great reading public – if infinitely nearer to the select few who have trained faculties of literary appre-ciation – than many a writer of far less worth. For the most part the reviewer finds it impossible to regret this, for the reason that the very mental attributes which may hedge Mr Conrad about with barriers where the crowd is concerned, are the qualities which make his work a permanent delight to the few, and a real addition to literature.

But, admitting all this, as we do, we yet find some legitimate ground for regret in the case of this book, and of, say, *Nostromo*. The writer of a 'simple tale' ought to show some regard for the simple reader, if not in the essen-tials of his story, certainly in the details of its construction. Mr Conrad's lordly disregard of such an element as time, for instance, is a little unkind to the simple reader. Two leading figures in the book are carrying on a highly interesting conversation, a dialogue vital to the story. In the midst we are stopped abruptly, and treated to

twenty pages of retrospective digression before the conversation is resumed. Again, a catastrophe occurs; the
lurid horror of the event is pictured for us by a master
hand. The skill of the writer hurries us on, but only, as
though for his amusement, to run our heads suddenly
against a blank wall in the dark. 'Now wait there,' says
the author, in effect, 'and I will tell you about a whole lot
of things that came before the catastrophe.' The writer's
craftsmanship is such that the critical reader excuses such
odd construction; but what of the good soul who sets out
to read for the story alone, as many will? In short, we
think Mr Conrad apt to be too arbitrary. Yet, in view of
the excellence of his work, which, regarded against a
background of average fiction, has the quality of a fine
diamond lying among shingle, we advise the ordinary
reader not to be discouraged by this.

The Secret Agent is a tale of life among foreign anarchists in London, and deals with a remarkable incident
in which a foreign embassy to the Court of St James's
deliberately provoked a dynamite outrage through a
secret agent of its own, by way of furthering its policy
in this country. It is a masterly study, the raw material
of which would have been turned into crude melodrama
by some writers. Mr Conrad has made it the vehicle
for some of the most telling characterization he has accomplished. His English is usually so scrupulously true and
sound that our attention is drawn by a couple of curiously
unfortunate phrases in *The Secret Agent* – on p. 311
[p. 220 of Dent Edition] : 'At any rate he risked consciously nothing more but arrest for him'; and on p. 315
[p. 222 of Dent Edition] : 'A youngish composer in
pass of becoming famous.' But there is hardly another
sentence which is not calculated to charm the reader of
discernment.

*

By the end of October Conrad summed up his disappointment in a letter to Galsworthy (24 October 1907):

The Secret Agent has run his little race with the moderate triumph of two editions. I go on with *Chance* convulsively as a jaded horse may be made to gallop, – and I fear it's all extravagant trash, – the trash and the extravagance of despair. Pages *must* be written, – so I write them, – and I haven't even the comfort to think I am writing them fast enough.

Early in the next year Conrad pronounced the final verdict, again in a letter to Galsworthy (6 January 1908):

The Secret Agent may be pronounced by now an honourable failure. It brought me neither love nor promise of literary success. I own that I am cast down. I suppose I am a fool to have expected anything else. I suppose there is something in me that is unsympathetic to the general public, – because the novels of Hardy, for instance, are generally tragic enough and gloomily written too, – and yet they have sold in their time and are selling to the present day.

Foreignness, I suppose.[5]

* * *

In the United States *The Secret Agent* was published by Harper and Brothers at $1.50. Its reception was much the same as in England. Though widely reviewed and usually with great respect, the book was not really liked. At least not often. The keynote was sounded by the distinguished New York weekly *The Nation*:

The Nation (New York), 26 September 1907

Mr Conrad (Joseph Conrad Korzeniowszi) has dis-

appointed some of his early admirers. On the strength of
his first stories, he was hailed as the coming novelist, a
man whose writing possessed both substance and style.
English was not his mother tongue, but he had mastered
it completely, and wrote with astonishing power. Some
of his descriptions, especially in his tales of the sea, stood
comparison with the work of Stevenson and Kipling. But
Nostromo was rather a heavy dose – prolix and in construction suggesting Browning's *The Ring and the Book*.
When you finally got through it, you felt that you had
read an impressive novel, but in many passages attention
flagged.

The Secret Agent is still less of a story. Mr Conrad is
fluent, almost too fluent. He is a master of striking phrase
and of mechanically admirable sentences. He offers us
some brilliant bits of description, but the narrative as a
whole does not move. It tells us of a secret agent employed
by the Russian Embassy in London, and of his relations
with his employers, with the police, the anarchists on
whom he spies, and the members of his own family. The
incidents are bomb-throwing, murder, and suicide – the
raw stuff of a shilling shocker. But the events are so over-
laid with description, analysis, and the study of the psychological side of the characters that the book is hard to
read. The characters stand forth clearly enough, but you
cannot get interested in them till you have gone through
the first half of the volume. This is too heavy a draft on
the faith of a reader.

*

In *The Dial*, a Chicago fortnightly that was not yet as
eminent as it was to become when it moved to New York
in 1918, William Morton Payne was equally dis-
appointed :

The Dial, 16 October 1907

We approach Mr Conrad's *The Secret Agent* with anticipations that are not fulfilled. Its programme of anarchists and bombs and detectives promises lively entertainment, but we get instead interminable descriptions and discussions of motive. The result is a good story completely smothered by analysis. Both analysis and characterization are exceedingly acute, for few men are Mr Conrad's equals in command of the incisive touch and the illuminating phrase. But a novel upon such a theme as this calls for action, and again action, and of this we get next to nothing. We hardly recall an equal disappointment since reading *The Princess Casamassima*. If the reader will make up his mind beforehand to look for nothing but psychological interest, he will find it aplenty. But the natural man in him must be prepared for shocks. He will be expected to remain unchafed while a dramatic conversation is indefinitely suspended until the author has freed his own capacious mind at great length, and, when the anarchist outrage which is the climax of the story actually comes off, he will be expected to hark back, and toil laboriously up to the climax a second time. These things are exasperating, of course, but they are inseparable from Mr Conrad's way of working, and those who have read his other books are fairly forewarned. In comparison with the bulk of this narrative, its grim closing chapters have an unexpected directness and concentration.

*

Some of us may find it in our hearts to be grateful for the phrase 'completely smothered by analysis' here, but the captious muddlement with which *The Secret Agent* was greeted by the *Boston Evening Transcript* was another matter :

Boston Evening Transcript, 9 October 1907

To pick up *The Secret Agent* with the expectation that it is a shilling shocker, even though it bears Joseph Conrad's name as author, would be a serious mistake. Nevertheless it contains the stuff whereof shilling shockers are made, but in Mr Conrad's developing hand it becomes something far different and far superior, even if less interesting. It is by no means a straightforward and uninterrupted narrative of events, and more than once in its course, since Mr Conrad is more expert as a psychologist than as a story-teller, the reader will be puzzled over the sequence of incidents and marvel at the exasperating course of an author whose method leads his characters into the most exasperating of chronological tangles. At one moment we are reading of Mr Verloc, the secret agent in London of a great European power. At another we see him at his home in a mean street of Soho, where he cloaks his profession under the part of shopkeeper. At another, we are introduced to an eccentric gang of so-called Anarchists, and again and again we see Mr Verloc here, there, and everywhere without the slightest regard to the logic of time or place or action.

What dramatic and narrative power there is in *The Secret Agent* is isolated and fragmentary, due more to Mr Conrad's exceptional power at the analysis of character and motive than to his skill as a teller of tales. It reveals to us the depths of the human personality as a separate entity, but it combines men and women in a way that is wholly impossible and almost irrational. There is nothing plausible in the story as a story, although there is

a great deal that is comprehensible and marvellously true
to life in the personages that give the story its reason and
its purpose. Various phases of London life are entered into
by Mr Conrad from the grandeur of Westminster to the
degradation of Soho, and now and then he attempts to
lighten the course of his story by an attempt at humor
that is a ghastly failure. His private secretary and his
Sir Ethelred are grotesquely impossible from any point
of view. When a novelist is thinking continuously of the
thoughts of his characters, as Mr Conrad is, he is certain
to produce a vague and incomprehensible effect. Words
and not deeds are too frequently Mr Conrad's resource,
just as the ordinary novelist is led astray by deeds instead
of by words. As a piece of intricate novel writing, as a
psychological study, *The Secret Agent* possesses strength
of purpose and accomplishment, but merely as a narrative – and Mr Conrad seems at times to be striving ener-
getically towards a narrative coherence – it is extremely
ineffective.

*

There were also, of course, some favourable reviews,
and among them two of particular interest, since they
hailed *The Secret Agent* as Conrad's finest work. At
least one English reviewer had already briefly expressed
this view, in *Outlook* :

Outlook, 16 November 1907

Mr Conrad's description of his story as 'a simple tale'
is true only in the sense that simplicity is the keynote of
his peculiar method. Both the personages and the action
of this grim tragedy are out of the ordinary, and yet we

are made to feel that the conclusions at which he arrives
are not only inevitable, but the only conclusions which
the circumstances could evolve. This is Mr Conrad's art.
He is a master of beautiful prose, and every word in his
narrative has its special appropriateness. But the effect
would be the same without these adventitious aids. The
events he relates are not suggestive of pre-ordained destiny, although their finality may recall the fatalism of a
Greek drama : they are just the logical results of given
circumstances acting upon certain temperaments. Thus
we can enter into the motive which led Verloc, government spy and seller of shady prints, to send the half-witted
Stevie on his fatal errand with the bomb; just as we can
sympathise with the passion of maternity which the child-
less wife of Verloc lavishes upon her idiot brother. And
so the killing of her husband with the kitchen knife does
not read like cold-blooded murder, but as the only thing
to be done in a hopeless *impasse*. The book is a masterpiece of elemental emotions. There is, of course, much
more in it – many little character sketches which are
inimitable in their way – but this dominant quality marks
it as the most remarkable piece of work that even Mr
Conrad has achieved.

*

Conrad could hardly have been as pleased with the even
briefer eulogy pronounced in Putman's 'Idle Notes of
an Idle Fellow' :

Putnam's Monthly, December 1907

Of the fiction that we have read in the course of the past
month, Joseph Conrad's story of *The Secret Agent*

(Harper) has interested us the most. This story-teller builds remarkable phrases. He has much music and as much power. His unfailing humor is very audaciously employed. He makes fun of his characters while he is leading them in the ways of tragedy. He gives us goose-flesh while he is amusing us. In an Idle Reader's opinion he is the best man at present telling stories.

*

The most gratifying tribute was that of the *New York Times Book Review*. Its headline ran :

JOSEPH CONRAD'S
LATEST AND BEST

'The Secret Agent' Fine Example of this Novelist's
Ability in Analysis
of Character.

New York Times Book Review, 21 September 1907

Mr Joseph Conrad is a specialist in the sombre. Also he is able to write of woman without investing her with a shred of romance. Therefore, he is cut off from the wider popular favor. But there is no man alive more able than he to transmute life into words, which, better read, are transmuted into life again. His method, it seems, is almost mechanical. He takes the human creature, composite of conscious and unconscious impulses, obscurely motived in the roots of being and the tangle of desires and associations, made more complex, but not controlled by that

reason which is to most men as a pilot house whose wheel
is inexpertly geared to the rudder – he takes this mysterious creature, analyses the part of each impulse in the
creature's external action, and then reconstructs the whole
upon white paper out of mere printed language in such
fashion that the stark humanity of it throws the multi-
tudinous detail – provided the reader has a fairly competent imagination – into the just perspective of real life.
In other words, the reader, for the time being, is endowed,
to his immense enlargement, with Mr Conrad's eyes and
insight: he sees and feels what Mr Conrad would see
and feel in the presence of the actuality. To compass this
thing is the artist's gift, and when we insist on the 'fairly
competent imagination' in the reader we are not sub-
tracting in the least from the artist's credit. So much imagination is the necessary complement of his own.

[*The body of the review develops this idea further. Here,
to cite another passage, is the treatment of the character
of Stevie.*]

The young man of little wit is naturally the other in-
mate of the house of Verloc. He has his part in the tragedy
also. Stevie, a creature of 'immoderate compassion, apt
to forget mere facts – his name and address, for instance
– had a faithful memory for sensations'. So, gazing upon
a cab horse of 'aspect profoundly lamentable' and informed by the cabman that he had to make the miserable
beast go because he needed the fares for his 'missus and
the kids at home', Stevie was near choked with grief and
indignation 'at one sort of wretchedness having to feed
upon the anguish of another, at the poor cabman beating
the poor horse in the name, as it were, of the poor kids
at home'. Mr Conrad discovers Stevie's processes even
further:

'The tenderness to all pain and misery, the desire to make the horse happy and the cabman happy, had reached the point of a bizarre longing to take them to bed with him. And that he knew was impossible. For Stevie was not mad. It was, as it were, a symbolic longing. At the same time it was very distinct,' because, 'when, as a child, he cowered in a dark corner, scared, wretched, sore, and miserable, his sister Winnie used to come along and carry him off to bed with her as if to a heaven of consoling peace.' Thus the mechanics of poor Stevie's 'anguish of immoderate compassion'. 'Shame!' he cried, at last. 'Stevie was no master of phrases, and, perhaps for that very reason, his thoughts lacked clearness and precision.'

Conversely, Mr Conrad, who is a master of phrases, and whose thoughts, even when the subject matter of them is elusive and complex beyond calculation, are both clear and precise. Therein is part of his mastery, but the secret of his real strength, one fancies, is just that sense of the potency of association in giving form to crude human impulses, which is shown in the bizarre mental symbol of Stevie's passionate tenderness. Later, Mr Conrad shows the working of other spells of association whose key is a phrase merely. Thus is a woman driven to her death and a man to madness. Figure to yourself the murderess flying through the night and the fog, haunted by the matter-of-fact words which in England are apt to conclude the brief newspaper account of an execution – 'The drop given was fourteen feet'. In such fashion is the terror of the gallows made concrete – it bores at the consciousness like a fly buzzing against a window pane.

NOTES

1. Jean-Aubry, *Life and Letters*, II 55.

2. Ibid. 56.

3. *Letters from Conrad: 1895 to 1924*, edited with Introduction and Notes by Edward Garnett (London : Nonesuch Press, 1928) pp. 211–12.

4. Ibid., p. 212.

5. Jean-Aubry, *Life and Letters*, II 63, 65.

In his first twelve years as a writer Conrad had won the
praise and friendship of many of the writers of the day;
but although, in addition to reviews, a number of articles
about him had appeared, none had been as important
as John Galsworthy's essay in 1908.

The two men had been friends before either was an
author, and their relations had been particularly close
during the writing of *The Secret Agent*. On 31 March
1906 Conrad wrote a review article praising *The Man
of Property* in *Outlook*; that summer Conrad's second son
was born in Galsworthy's house, and was named John;
and at the time of the appearance of *The Secret Agent*
Galsworthy wrote an essay about Conrad of which he
sent a draft for comment. Conrad replied:

Joseph Conrad to John Galsworthy, 29 October 1907

The reading of your article soothed my spirit of profound
discontent. The thing is magnificently all right in its general
considerations. As to their application to my personality,
it is not for me to say. A too protesting modesty would be
uncivil to you. To show all my gratification would be perhaps indecent. But since your friendship is too sincere to
deal in anything but truth, I will tell you that I am glad the
truth is *this* and no other. There are sentences I would bind
about my brow like a laurel wreath and rest content.

I won't say any more just now. I want to come very soon
and talk to you. I would ask you at once to eliminate the
word aristocracy, when you see the proof. The name has

never been illustrated by a senatorial dignity, which was
the only basis of Polish aristocracy. The Equestrian Order
is more the thing. Land-tilling gentry is the most precise
approach to a definition of my modest origin. As English
publications reach far and wide notwithstanding the Censorship [in Poland], I am anxious not to be suspected of
the odious ridicule of passing off myself for what I am not.
I'll talk to you more of that when we meet. The correction
I ask for will spoil the sentence as it stands : but in that
respect I may express the doubt whether ship-life, though
pervaded by a sort of rough equality is truly democratic
in its real essence. . . .[1]

Other minor corrections follow, which seem to have been
incorporated into the final text. It appeared the next
April and is reprinted below on pp. 89–98.

To the modern reader Galsworthy's eulogy may seem
of largely historical interest. It certainly reminds us of how
much loftier was the Edwardian notion of critical style
than that customary today. Galsworthy, in this much
like Conrad as a critic, writes in terms of such cosmic
generality that we find it difficult to be sure that he is
actually talking about anything in particular. Yet if we
can penetrate the surface of his special rhetorical decorum, Galsworthy is essentially dealing with some of the
basic critical issues raised by Conrad and *The Secret
Agent*. Conrad's irony, for instance, certainly comes from
his sense of the inequality of the endless contest between
the 'unethical morality of Nature' and mankind's need
to impose upon the natural world an imaginary order
more gratifying to his pride and his laziness.

Galsworthy's reputation was only beginning in 1908,
but his essay remained the most influential critical estimate of Conrad until the appearance in 1914 of the first
full-length monograph, Richard Curle's *Joseph Conrad:
A Study*.

Curle had made Conrad's acquaintance through an earlier essay, published in 1912; and with a characteristic combination of polite reserve and effusive encouragement, Conrad had helped Curle in the preparation of the book. Its general aim was to rescue Conrad from the now-established stereotype of the Polish seaman who wrote *Lord Jim*. Curle compared Conrad with other major English novelists – Hardy, Meredith, James – and with the great Europeans, so as to establish his view that it was through Conrad that 'England first enters the "tradition" of Continental literature' and ranks with 'the great French and Russian Realists'.[2]

Curle regarded *The Secret Agent* as one of Conrad's major works. *Nostromo* was 'by far his greatest [novel] . . . a phenomenal masterpiece . . . Conrad's genius incarnate'; *Chance* was 'the most finished of his books'; while *Under Western Eyes*, though 'a surer piece of art' than *The Secret Agent*, was 'not to be placed on so lofty a pinnacle'. Curle's study, however, is organised in chapters on such general topics as 'Conrad's Atmosphere', 'Conrad as Psychologist', so that there is no comprehensive analysis of *The Secret Agent*, or indeed of any single work. Curle explains the unpopularity of *The Secret Agent* on three main grounds. It 'outraged' the image of Conrad that his earlier works had set up; it did not, like the novels of Wells and Galsworthy, deal with the problems of 'righting the world'; and it was also outside the tradition of the 'English novels of character'.[3]

As regards this last problem, Curle asserts that Conrad makes character 'subordinate to the unity of the book' as a whole; Conrad is more interested in 'the changing complex of human relations' than in people 'as individuals'; and his psychology typically concentrates on 'personality (which is the impression created by a figure on other people's minds)' rather than on 'character (which is what a figure really is)'.[4]

Curle's treatment of the characters in *The Secret Agent* is not very full. Verloc is a typical Conrad creation in that, like Almayer, Jim or Charles Gould, he is a man dominated by an '*idée fixe*' – in his case 'comfort of mind and body'. Curle's most unfamiliar opinion of the characters concerns Stevie:

A very marked sympathy and intuition have been lavished on Stevie's portrait – and lavished, I should suspect, not alone for his sake but for the sake of making us comprehend the relationship of Stevie and his sister. For her devotion to him is that of a boundless maternal pity for the innocent helplessness of a child, and in that emotion we see him as he really is – the pathetic fragment of a beautiful and trusting nature. For Stevie's mind is only warped in its lack of growth, it is not warped at all in any quality of true humanity. Its secretiveness and its openness alike represent the temperament of a sensitive boy.[5]

So sentimental an interpretation may strike us as largely contradicted by the cold irony through which Stevie is presented. Conrad surely sees Stevie's sensitiveness to suffering in exactly the same impartial perspective as everything else in his black comedy of human cross-purposes. Curle, indeed, later comes close to saying as much when he comes to deal with Conrad's irony. It is essentially a means of impersonal aesthetic distancing; and it makes the reader feel that Conrad is 'a mere watcher leaving his characters to fight out alone with fate the battle of good and evil, of purpose and futility'.[6]

Among Curle's other judgements two are of particular interest. On Winnie Verloc, he is rather unconventional. Far from being unable to understand women, Conrad's feminine portraits are, Curle asserts, his 'most finished, delicate and poignant'. Curle also makes some illuminating comments on *The Secret Agent* as 'a triumph of atmosphere' : Conrad shows his originality even in the treatment of inanimate objects; and Curle instances the piano in the Silenus beer-hall among the objects which live for the reader 'in the emotion of the story with a kind of crooked vitality of their own'.[7]

Curle concluded that 'Conrad's day is at hand and that once his sun has risen it will not set'.[8] Though the book itself was given very unfavourable reviews, Curle's prophecy proved to be correct. The next year saw an appreciable increase in critical acclaim for Conrad. In England, Hugh Walpole wrote a brief but highly favourable monograph, which was also published in the United States. There chapters on Conrad had begun to appear in books about modern literature as early as 1912. In 1915 Wilson Folett's *Joseph Conrad: A Short Study* appeared; and in 1916 William Lyon Phelps lent his considerable academic authority to support Conrad's acknowledged eminence by devoting some twenty-five pages to him in his book on *The Advance of the English Novel*. The most influential American enthusiast, however, was probably H. L. Mencken, whose *A Book of Prefaces* appeared in 1917. It opened with a long essay on Conrad whose tenor may be gathered from the following extract :

My own conviction, sweeping all those reaches of living fiction that I know, is that Conrad's figure stands out from the field like the Alps from the Piedmont plain. He not only has no masters in the novel; he has scarcely a colourable peer. Perhaps Thomas Hardy and Anatole France – old men both, their work behind them. But who else? James is dead. Meredith is dead. So is George Moore, though he lingers on. So are all the Russians of the first rank; Andrieff, Gorki and their like are light cavalry. In Sudermann,

Germany has a writer of short stories of very high calibre, but where is the German novelist to match Conrad? Clara Viebig? Thomas Mann? Gustav Frenssen? Arthur Schnitzler? Surely not! As for the Italians, they are either absurd tear-squeezers or more absurd harlequins. As for the Spaniards and the Scandinavians, they would pass for geniuses only in Suburbia. In America, setting aside an odd volume here and there, one can discern only Dreiser – and of Dreiser's limitations I shall discourse anon. There remains England. England has the best second-raters in the world; nowhere else is the general level of novel writing so high; nowhere else is there a corps of journeyman novelists comparable to Wells, Bennett, Benson, Walpole, Beresford, George, Galsworthy, Hichens, De Morgan, Miss Sinclair, Hewlett and company. They have a prodigious facility; they know how to write; even the least of them is, at all events, a more competent artisan than, say, Dickens, or Bulwer-Lytton, or Sienkiewicz, or Zola. But the literary *grande passion* is simply not in them. They get nowhere with their suave and interminable volumes. Their view of the world and its wonders is narrow and superficial. They are, at bottom, no more than clever mechanicians.

As Galsworthy has said, Conrad lifts himself immeasurably above them all. One might well call him, if the term had not been cheapened into cant, a cosmic artist. His mind works upon a colossal scale; he conjures up the general out of the particular. What he sees and describes in his books is not merely this man's aspiration or that woman's destiny, but the overwhelming sweep and devastation of universal forces, the great central drama that is at the heart of all other dramas, the tragic struggles of the soul of man under the gross stupidity and obscene joking of the gods.[9]

After the end of the war there was a boom in Conrad. A series of lavish collected editions came out; complete translations were under way in France and Poland; while in 1923 a sensational sale of manuscripts in the Anderson auction galleries in New York fetched unprecedentedly high prices.

Inevitably the amount of writing about Conrad also increased rapidly. Most of it was journalistic – largely biographical and anecdotal. In keeping with this trend the main critical emphasis remained on the tales of the sea, and *The Secret Agent* was relatively neglected. The generally accepted view was that expressed earlier in Hugh Walpole's book: Conrad's major works were *The Nigger of the Narcissus, Lord Jim*, the stories in the *Youth* volume, and *Nostromo. The Secret Agent* began the new phase of Conrad's career; in his later novels he had become more detached, and in this *The Secret Agent* was typical. As Walpole put it, the novel was the work of 'a finer artist', but had 'lost something of that earlier compelling interest'.[10]

NOTES

1. Jean-Aubry, *Life and Letters*, II 63–4.
2. Richard Curle, *Joseph Conrad: A Study* (London, 1914) p. 233.
3. Ibid., pp. 40, 47, 45, 6, 7.
4. Ibid., pp. 96, 110.
5. Ibid., pp. 95, 135.
6. Ibid., p. 163.
7. Ibid., pp. 145, 74, 216.
8. Ibid., p. 13.
9. H. L. Mencken, *A Book of Prefaces* (New York, 1917) pp. 61–3.
10. Hugh Walpole, *Joseph Conrad* (London, 1915) p. 19.

4 MODERN CRITICISM: GENERAL TRENDS

Conrad's death on 3 August 1924 brought forth a flood of tributes. Of these Ford Madox Ford's *Joseph Conrad: A Personal Remembrance* (London and Boston, 1924) is by all odds the most important. Though unreliable in many of its facts, it conveys a vivid and authentic sense of Conrad the man, and of the nature of the collaboration between him and Ford. Ford greatly admired *The Secret Agent*; but neither here nor in his other volumes of reminiscence does he say much about it critically.

In the 1920s the two most significant treatments of *The Secret Agent* were probably Hugh Walpole's essay on it in *A Conrad Memorial Library: The Collection of George T. Keating* (New York, 1929), and Thomas Mann's introduction to a German translation in 1926. Both essays, reprinted below, are more interesting for their incidental perceptions and judgements than for any very closely argued critical analysis. For Walpole the ride in the cab is 'one of the great things in English literature'; while for Mann, who, like Walpole, reserves his most unqualified admiration for Conrad the seaman, *The Secret Agent* is particularly significant in the light of the ideological pressures in Germany during the Weimar Republic. From the perspective of a country torn between traditional Western liberal ideas and the apocalyptic moral and political possibilities held out by Russian literature and politics, by Dostoevsky and Bolshevism, Mann finds Conrad's 'untrammelled objectivity' as a narrator to be essentially committed to the 'liberating task' of expressing Conrad's Western 'passion for freedom'.

A popular edition of *The Secret Agent* appeared in England in 1927. There was no other new publication of the novel, apart from a new Uniform Cheap Edition begun by Dent in 1939, for over twenty years after Conrad's death, until the paperback revolution finally made it cheaply available on both sides of the Atlantic. During the 1930s Conrad's pessimistic conservatism was distinctly out of key with the prevailingly radical ideology; and what interest there was tended to concentrate on works such as *Heart of Darkness*, which could be read as attacks on the brutalities of colonialism, or, more widely, as predictions of the collapse of Western civilisation, as T. S. Eliot had used it in his epigraph to 'The Hollow Men' (1925) – 'Mistah Kurtz – he dead'.

The most interesting critical study of the 1930s was probably Edward Crankshaw's *Joseph Conrad: Some Aspects of the Art of the Novel* (London, 1936). Continuing the preoccupation of Henry James, and of his disciple Percy Lubbock in *The Craft of Fiction* (1921), Crankshaw gave the question of narrative point of view a central importance. His general critical judgement was that Conrad, 'Henry James apart, has done more than any other English novelist to put the English novel on its legs'. As regards *The Secret Agent*, Crankshaw showed how the narrator's ironic perspective 'contains' the commenting and universalising functions which Conrad elsewhere secured through Marlow; but the particular problems of *The Secret Agent* had called for a greater degree of distance from the characters, and a greater freedom of comment. Crankshaw concluded that in *The Secret Agent* Conrad 'achieved what may have been the greatest of all his purely technical feats'.[1]

For Henry James the First World War had made 'all the past . . . seem now a long treachery, an unthinkable humbug' (to William Roughead, 30 September 1914).

The Second World War showed that the First was not just an accident, and that there was little reason to reject Conrad, as D. H. Lawrence had done in a letter to Garnett in 1912, on the grounds that he was one of 'the Writers among the Ruins'.[2] Ruins had become part of the landscape, and in 1945 Conrad's view of life was found to have survived not merely intact, but with commanding topicality. Disillusionment with the whole progressive political heritage, and demoralising habituation to the sordid duplicities of the Cold War, prepared the general atmosphere; and at the same time the literary situation was correspondingly more favourable. One sign of this was that, among the most popular writers in England and America, two at least – Graham Greene and William Faulkner – were obvious disciples. They were even, indeed, disciples on occasion of that vein of ironic melodrama in Conrad of which *The Secret Agent* is the purest example.

If it was after the First World War that the Conrad boom had started among journalists and bibliophiles, it was really only after the Second that the boom began among the critics and scholars – so much so indeed that, from now on, this review of criticism of *The Secret Agent* will have no time to mention general books or essays on Conrad, but only specific studies of the novel, and even then only a small selection of them.

The most important single work in starting the postwar vogue both of Conrad and of *The Secret Agent* was undoubtedly F. R. Leavis's *The Great Tradition*, published in 1948. Leavis pronounced defiantly: 'Jane Austen, George Eliot, Henry James, Conrad, and D. H. Lawrence: the great tradition of the English novel is *there*.' Having promoted Conrad above Fielding, Scott, Thackeray, Meredith, Hardy and Joyce, Leavis went on to an extremely influential revaluation of the main works in the Conrad canon. *Lord Jim* was presented as minor, *Heart of Darkness* as flawed, while, along with *Nostromo*, *The Secret Agent* was proclaimed 'one of Conrad's two supreme masterpieces, one of the two unquestionable classics of the first order that he added to the English novel'.[3]

Since Leavis the critical attitude to *The Secret Agent* has usually been much more favourable. One exception may be briefly noted here: Irving Howe in his *Politics and the Novel* (1953). For Howe, Conrad's treatment of anarchism, and indeed of politics generally in *The Secret Agent*, seemed blind and imperceptive, especially when compared with *Nostromo*, which Howe, in common with most liberal and Marxist critics, sees as a convincing and indeed prophetic vision of the historical and social processes of the modern world. On the other hand two other more recent critics, Leo Gurko and Eloise Knapp Hay, strongly endorse Conrad's sociological and political insight in *The Secret Agent*.

It was virtually impossible to categorise briefly the great variety of recent critical approaches to *The Secret Agent* with any degree of justice. But one can at least venture that, compared with earlier criticism, its characteristic emphasis has been exegetic rather than evaluative. The formalist or New Critical is the clearest example of the purely exegetic approach. It attempts to elucidate the internal relationships of the literary work, considered as an autonomous entity quite separate from its author, its historical situation or its relationship to the outside world. But – whether because Conrad doesn't lend himself to such an approach, or because the formalists have not been attracted to Conrad – there is little strictly formalist writing on *The Secret Agent*.

A somewhat similar approach, however, was used by John Hagan Jr in his article 'The Design of Conrad's *The Secret Agent*';[4] and E. M. W. Tillyard's essay, *'The*

Secret Agent Reconsidered', belongs to a related but much older mode of criticism, since an appeal to the notion of formal literary criteria underlies his judgement that *The Secret Agent* 'hovers a little uneasily between a novel in the grand manner and the long short-story'.

During the last decade the formalist approach in general has been much less popular than other, somewhat less purely exegetic, tendencies. Three of them are represented below, and may be tentatively classified as the symbolical, the phenomenological or existential, and the psychological.

One relatively pure example of the symbolical approach is Robert W. Stallman's 'Time and *The Secret Agent*'. Stallman's basic presupposition can be inferred from his statement that *The Secret Agent* is 'one of the most cryptographic works in all British fiction'. His analysis pays a good deal of attention to such matters as the prevalence of circles in various forms; and this is part of his general argument that the attack on Greenwich Observatory is to be viewed as essentially a symbolic attempt at 'the destruction of space and time'.

Many other recent critics are symbolical in a much less esoteric way. They do not restrict themselves to structure and literal meaning, and they go beyond or behind the words on the page; but they do so not in quest of cryptographic interpretations, but because they are interested in interpreting and evaluating literature according to certain presuppositions about the nature of reality. Thus Avrom Fleishman's 'The Symbolic World of *The Secret Agent*' synthesises a metaphysical world-view out of the details of Conrad's text; and though this view is arrived at by seeing characters, actions and background as representative of larger realities, the final interpretation, though more general, is not contrary to the literal meaning.

No good critic, of course, can be reduced to a simple category; and though Fleishman's technique of analysis is primarily symbolic, what his analysis discovers also suggests the influence of phenomenology.

Phenomenology is primarily an epistemology which is opposed to naturalism, and which maintains that the only valid approach to truth is through the individual consciousness. The application of phenomenology to literary criticism therefore involves describing the way an individual consciousness – usually that of the author – sees and experiences itself and the external world. This approach is not, of course, entirely new, since much older criticism has the author's vision of life as its main subject; but the phenomenologists are more conscious and explicit about their aims. Fleishman, for example, entitles the three sections of his essay 'The Moral World', 'The Physical World' and 'Space and Time'.

Phenomenological and existential philosophy have much in common. Both start from the individual consciousness as the primary reality, and both deny the existence of any objective or external standards of judgement. But whereas the phenomenologists use such neutral categories of analysis as space and time, and make no assumptions about the actual content of experience, the existentialists share various broad assumptions about the human condition. They assume, for example, that men, unlike animals, have no fixed relationship with the natural, the social or the religious world. Facing this separateness and meaninglessness, men have to become aware of the absurdity of their condition before they can create their own personal essence, and give a meaning to their lives.

J. Hillis Miller is a theoretically sophisticated critic whose general position is phenomenological, and much of his analysis of *The Secret Agent* is concerned with seeing how the individual consciousnesses of the characters are seen to operate, and how Conrad's narration supplies a further subjective dimension to the novel's vision of the world. On the other hand, what Hillis Miller finds to be the main content of *The Secret Agent* is typically existentialist. His essay occurs in a study of what he calls *Poetry of Reality* – Yeats, Dylan Thomas, Wallace Stevens and William Carlos Williams. Each of these poets is seen as having first experienced life as a total void or darkness, and as having then created a vision which went beyond his initial nihilism. The long introductory chapter deals with Conrad, and particularly with *Heart of Darkness* and *The Secret Agent*. Both of these, in Hillis Miller's view, are works in which Conrad, by submerging his reader in darkness and chaos and destroying the illusions about his importance in the universe which flatter or sustain him, prefigures the essential movement of the modern consciousness.

Another recent critical approach to *The Secret Agent* may be described as psychological. Here again the term needs some explanation, since many other critics could also be called psychological. V. S. Pritchett, for example, is a psychological critic in the broad sense that, as a practising novelist, he has a genius for penetrating diagnosis of a literary work as an expression of a particular temperament. The criticism of Albert Guérard, on the other hand, is psychological in the more technical and specialised sense that a particular theory, in his case Jungian, provides the prevailing assumptions by which particular works are interpreted and assessed. Guérard's essay on *The Secret Agent* occurs in what is surely the best single critical study of Conrad. Guérard does not find in *The Secret Agent* any 'deep introspective drive . . . or author-identification'; it is not, like *Heart of Darkness* or 'The Secret Sharer', an expression of unconscious forces; and so the novel, for all its brilliance, is found to be cold, unilluminating, minor.

There is a similar lack of enthusiasm for *The Secret Agent* in several of the other critics, not represented here, whose approach is psychological in a technical sense. Thus Thomas Moser, in his important study of the much-mooted question of Conrad's literary decline in his last ten or fifteen years, assumes that Conrad's own psycho-sexual life was deeply maimed by his childhood experiences. He sees *The Secret Agent* as a borderline work, half belonging to the later period of Conrad's literary development when, in order to be more popular, he attempted to deal with sexual matters, on whose treatment his own phobias and inadequacies had a crippling effect. Moser finds Winnie 'a memorable female character'; but she is too limited to be more than 'a minor triumph', and lacks 'the moral and psychological complexity which informs Conrad's greatest creations'.[5]

Norman Holland, in his recent 'Style as Character: *The Secret Agent*', interprets the ironic style of the novel as a psychic defence against what, following Guérard, Holland takes to be an enduring conflict in Conrad between the conformist seaman and the nihilistic outlaw. The novel is essentially about Conrad's characteristic preoccupation – the conflicts between the controllers and the controlled, between the police and the anarchists; but Conrad's ironic style acts as a censoring device, preventing Conrad from any unconscious identification with the destructive and negative forces in the novel, and at the same time enabling him to remain superior to the pitifully inadequate representatives of the established moral, social and political order.

The difficulty with such analyses is that they depend on our accepting the critic's way of interpreting Conrad's own psyche in terms of a particular theoretical model of the human mind. Thus those who, like Guérard and Claire Rosenfeld, adopt a basically Jungian point of view tend to give a privileged status to whatever action or symbols express the darker, and unconscious or mythic, side of human experience, while those who, like Moser, incline to more orthodox Freudian views make a great deal of whatever in the novels fails to come up to some assumed standard of mature heterosexuality in character and personal relationships.

Both kinds of psychological critic are, paradoxically enough, at cross-purposes with the existential or pheno- menological interpretation of *The Secret Agent*, since it is the very blackness of Conrad's vision of human defeat which makes Guérard and Moser condemn the novel and which constitutes its validity for Fleishman and Hillis Miller. The divergence presumably arises from their dif- ferent assumptions about what the controlling conscious- ness of the novel really is. For Fleishman and Hillis Miller it is the total consciousness operating in the work – Conrad's mind and its comprehensive diagnosis of the metaphysical absurdity of the modern world; for the psychological critics it is the characters in the novel, and they are nearly all maimed, frustrated and grotesquely deviant people.

If we turn to the most recent biography of Conrad, Bernard C. Meyer's *Joseph Conrad: A Psychoanalytic Biography* (1967), we can find a wealth of clinical ex- planations for this. Conrad's early years, Meyer assumes, left him with an unendurable legacy of abnormal impulses and repressions, from oral aggression to hair fetishism. In particular *The Secret Agent* expresses Conrad's latent impulses to infanticide, arising from his wish to mono- polise all feminine and maternal attention. As Meyer writes: 'during [his wife's] second pregnancy he appears to have dealt with these impulses through the medium of artistic sublimation, for it was during those months that he composed *The Secret Agent*, a story in which a "father" causes a small child to be blown to bits'.[6]

Conrad was no doubt a much more curious and difficult man than appeared in the earlier accounts of him by his admirers; and there is certainly something odd about the fact, recounted by Meyer,[7] that in the twenty-five stories in Conrad where the plot involves the protagonist with a woman, seventeen of the heroes die — often, as with Verloc, at the hands of the woman; in the six tales dealing only with men, however, the hero survives. Yet there are many difficulties involved in accepting such interpretations, quite apart from any intuitive protest that they may be unconscious strategies of impertinent patronage on the part of the critic. Most obviously, we do not have the evidence we need to be able to reconstruct Conrad's inner life adequately; and what literary evidence there is, is in itself highly problematic. There is doubtless, as many critics have said, a great deal of emphasis in *The Secret Agent* on gross physical appetite. But it is doubtful whether Meyer strengthens his case for Conrad's oral sadism by pointing out that the anarchist Yundt labels 'the present social conditions . . . cannibalistic', or by italicising the fact that 'Winnie had been in love with a young impecunious *butcher*'.[8]

The most important objection, of course, is 'So what?' Does the asserted psychopathology of the writer affect the truth of his picture of life? Even if we accept Meyer's view of Conrad the man, or of the clinical importance of some aspects of the novels, do the unconscious roots of Conrad's vision substantially deform the truth of the picture of human life which he arrived at in *The Secret Agent*?

On this matter, of course, the reader must judge for himself. The extracts above, and the various writings included in Part Two, are very far from exhausting the critical issues raised by *The Secret Agent*. All they can do is help to make us more aware of things in the novel which we might not otherwise have noticed, or, having noticed, have taken no further account of because they did not, at the time, fit into our own personal sense of the book as it developed.

NOTES

1. Edward Crankshaw, *Joseph Conrad: Some Aspects of the Art of the Novel* (London, 1936) pp. 164, 162.

2. Anthony Beal (ed.), *Selected Literary Criticism* (London, 1955) p. 132.

3. F. R. Leavis, *The Great Tradition* (London, 1948) pp. 27, 220.

4. For the facts of publication of this and other articles cited, but not reprinted, see the Select Bibliography.

5. Thomas Moser, *Joseph Conrad: Achievement and Decline* (Cambridge, Mass.: Harvard U.P., 1957) pp. 90, 92.

6. Bernard C. Meyer, *Joseph Conrad: A Psychoanalytic Biography* (Princeton U.P., 1967) p. 128.

7. Ibid., pp. 273–5.

8. Ibid., p. 189.

5 SOME OTHER CRITICAL ISSUES

There is one other important question which, as it seems
to me, is not satisfactorily answered in the body of critical
writing about *The Secret Agent*. How is it that a tale so
deeply depressing on the face of it, a tale in which every
possible card is stacked against human freedom and happiness, should be, for some readers at least, tonic rather
than depressive in its final effect?

Conrad's initial strategy, of course, is to dash all our
expectations. Picking up a book about a secret agent we
expect to find a hero who, happily unlike ourselves, knows
both how the social mechanism works and how to mani-
pulate it for his own gratification. Instead Conrad gives
us someone who understands even less than we do; and
instead of perfectly engineered encounters with ruthless
killers and beautiful spies, we are given a married man
who hardly notices that his wife is murdering him. If
Conrad were writing a parody of the espionage romance,
that would be amusing too; but just as we are denied the
pleasure of melodrama – there is no one we particularly want to applaud or hiss – so we are denied the
pleasures of parody or satire – the characters are too
human for that. And yet they are all, as Conrad put it in
a letter to his French translator Davray (8 November
1906), '*imbéciles*'.[1]

In so writing, Conrad was partly being ironically dis-
missive out of modesty about his own creation; but he
certainly also intended to emphasise that none of the
characters either understand themselves, or really know
what they are doing. In a sense this is Kafka's subject.
People feel lost because they apparently have no idea of

what the appropriate norms of feeling and action are. Seen from inside, and with the total identification that Kafka's narrative point of view evokes for his protagonists, we experience the terrors of being caught up in a paranoid fear of the world outside. Unlike Kafka, however, Conrad does not present his protagonists from within but from without; from this distant perspective we can observe that no one in *The Secret Agent* acts or thinks according to what the author or ourselves could regard as appropriate norms, but that – again unlike Kafka – no one individual is persecuted for it. In the world of *The Secret Agent* any punishment, like any other clear idea or normal feeling, is in effect quite irrelevant to the actual muddle in which humanity is inextricably immersed; and once the reader has measured this intractable reality, all he can do is, in T. S. Eliot's words, 'Wipe your hand across your mouth, and laugh'.

Laugh, certainly, not with the characters, nor even at them, but at the omnipresent discrepancy between pretence and reality. In his *The Tragic Vision* (1960) Murray Krieger argues that in such works as *Lord Jim, Nostromo* and *Victory* Conrad created a tragic vision of life; but though his protagonists were faced with grand and irreconcilable conflicts, neither they nor their circumstances enabled them to rise to the level of tragic action : Lord Jim, Decoud and Heyst in effect all find a form of suicide the only way out. Another way for Conrad to negotiate the conflict between the ideal and the actual in his gloomy vision was comic style. And it is surely this consistently comic style that characterises *The Secret Agent*, from the brilliant description of Verloc's walk to the Embassy in chap. 2, to that of the murder itself. To define the varying elements of this style is one task which the critics do not yet seem to have attempted; but it is surely the means whereby *The Secret Agent* seems modern in the way that Yeats, Eliot and Joyce are. All of them assume that it is the artist's voice alone which can impose some order on the vulgar folly of the modern world.

Such a line of argument is, of course, open to a serious objection, since it is an extreme version of the formalist position which assumes that works of art are autonomous creations, the nature of whose correspondence to the real world is irrelevant to the critic. To put it another way, to argue that *The Secret Agent* is a masterpiece of a special comic style is really to assert either that it is not, in the simplest sense, true, or else that its truth does not matter.

But to some of us at least the question of the truth of Conrad's fictional world is surely the most important question of all. It is not, certainly, the literal truth of a Naturalist or Realist novel; it is more a matter of how essential truths emerge from a consistent contrast between what is reported, and how.

In the present state of civilisation we must be very sure of our grounds before we reject what Conrad reports about the life of man in the modern city: an unimaginably dark chaos whose most evident features are blind cruelty, senseless violence, mutual unawareness and overpowering apathy. Yet even that life does have order of a kind, and one that persists. Not because man is governed by intelligence or responsibility; in the end neither Chief Inspector Heat nor the Assistant Commissioner has any more effect upon 'the street full of men' than either the anarchists or the reforming politicians who want to change it. Instead, all the various efforts to move the masses cancel each other out: the death of Verloc leaves Heat and Vladimir and the Professor undisturbed; and no one even knows what actually happened. In the vast scale of our society, it seems, anger and evil have no more final efficacy than laziness or love; all are muffled and distorted, like the sounds made in the Marabar caves in Forster's *A Passage to India*; and what finally emerges is the monotonous and meaningless but persistent hum of the street full of men.

We must make what we can of Conrad's closing suggestion that this sound, at least, will endure. It will certainly not inspire us to any great personal or political advance; and so even if we agree that the conclusion is true, it hardly seems bracing. This might be a fair, if crude, verdict on *The Trial*. It is not so as a verdict on *The Secret Agent* because the tension between what is seen and how it is presented betokens an admirable elasticity of spirit. The style of *The Secret Agent* expresses, not protective censorship, as Holland and Moser have suggested, but a control that approaches serenity. It asserts that whatever we see through it has been selected and reshaped, and invites us to join in the process whereby Conrad, in the novel where he took his closest and darkest look at modern urban civilisation, managed not to be overwhelmed. Like Mark Tapley, Conrad claims some credit for telling the truth and yet remaining, in his own peculiar way, quite cheerful.

NOTE

1. G. Jean-Aubry (ed.), *Lettres françaises* (Paris, 1929) pp. 77–9.

The Secret Agent may be said to exist in six versions: manuscript; serial; book; two dramatised forms; and the film.

(i) Conrad's complete manuscript, of 637 pages, is now in the Phillip H. and A. S. W. Rosenbach Foundation Museum and Library, in Philadelphia. It is not, unfortunately, available for reproduction except for short passages: one page may be seen, for example, in Eloise Knapp Hay's *The Political Novels of Joseph Conrad* (p. 231).

(ii) This manuscript was the basis of the serial version, which ran to eleven weekly numbers in *Ridgway's Militant Weekly* from 6 October to 15 December 1906. The serial was arranged in only six chapters: partly because, although the first four coincided with the present chaptering, chaps. 5 and 6 were much longer and took up most of the last seven issues; and partly because for the book form Conrad expanded the original last four chapters from the 3,500 words of the serial to over 31,000.[1]

(iii) The main differences between the serial and book forms of *The Secret Agent* have been studied in some detail, by Walter F. Wright in his *Romance and Tragedy in Joseph Conrad*, and by Harold E. Davis in his article 'Conrad's Revisions of *The Secret Agent*: A Study in Literary Impressionism'.

Wright concentrates on the changes in characterisation and narrative development. The main additions to the characterisation concerned Winnie, Heat and the Assistant Commissioner, although Conrad also sharpened the presentation of many other characters. Michaelis, for instance, became more of a humbug, the Professor more disinterested, Vladimir more urbane. There were in addition a few changes of name : Karl Yundt only received his appropriate baptism in the book, his serial name being Max Kling; while the too cosy appellation of Minnie in the serial became Winnie. As to the action, the main addition was the completely new chap. 10, in which the Assistant Commissioner reports to Sir Ethelred and gives Vladimir a veiled warning. This was only a part of the great expansion of the last four chapters, in which Conrad presented Winnie's mind and her relationship to Verloc much more fully, and made both her suicide and Ossipon's subsequent demoralisation much clearer.[2]

Davis mainly concentrates on the addition of exact concrete details to make characters and atmosphere more vivid. The physical characterisations of the cab driver (p. 157) or of Mrs Neale (p. 180) do not exist at all in the serial; nor do such significant contributions to the novel's atmosphere as the last sentence of chap. 9 (p. 213), or the last paragraph of chap. 4 (p. 79).

All these kinds of change may be studied further by comparing the last four chapters in the novel as it now stands, with the serial version.

(iv) Conrad, like Henry James, made several efforts at the glory and financial prizes to be obtained in the theatre, and with equal lack of success.[3] His dramatisation of *The Secret Agent* exists in two forms, that in four acts privately printed in 1921, and that in three acts which was produced at the Ambassadors' Theatre on 2 November 1922. The play was not successful, and ran only to 11 November. It failed with most of the critics, as well as with the public. On this Conrad wrote: 'The adverse reception by the critics . . . affected me not at all. I was amused by their touching unanimity in damning the play. It was like a chorus of parrots. . . .'[4]

The play followed the novel closely, and used much of the dialogue. The necessities of staging, however, meant that the action had to be concentrated in a few places. In the first scene, for example, we do not see Verloc walking through London and being received at the Embassy; instead, and rather inappropriately, Vladimir comes to the Verloc back parlour. Act II has three scenes, which occur in the Silenus, in the Assistant Commissioner's office, and in Lady Mabel's drawing-room. Act III has four scenes, which shift between the Verlocs' parlour and their shop. The murder of Verloc takes place in the parlour after the curtain has fallen; then Winnie reappears in the shop. Ossipon gets the pocket-book, and then, shaken by the sight of Verloc's corpse, and terrified of Winnie, tries to escape, is arrested, and at the end of the play is about to be taken off to prison for the murder of Verloc, while Winnie, helplessly deranged, crouches on the floor.

The essential difference between the novel and the play, of course, is the absence of the writer's ironic commentary. Conrad refers to this in the Author's Note to *The Secret Agent*: 'lately, circumstances . . . have compelled me to strip this tale of the literary robe of indignant scorn it has cost me so much to fit on it decently, years ago. I have been forced, so to speak, to look upon its bare bones. I confess that it makes a grisly skeleton.'

(v) Conrad was also interested in the cinema, and indeed collaborated with Pinker on a film scenario of 'Gaspar Ruiz', which is in the Yale University Library. He would have appreciated the irony that, because Hitchcock had already made a film called *The Secret Agent*, based on Somerset Maugham's Ashenden stories, Hitchcock's 1936 version of *The Secret Agent* had to be given another name – *Sabotage* in England and *A Woman*

Alone in the United States.[5] The scenario and setting were
very different from Conrad's. Verloc (Oscar Homolka)
manages a small cinema, and Heat employs a handsome
detective (John Loder) who courts Winnie (Sylvia Sidney) so that he can keep an eye on Verloc. There is a
somewhat improbable happy ending: a timely explosion
after the murder destroys the evidence against Winnie,
who then finds happiness in the detective's arms.

As a film *Sabotage* is, as Hitchcock remarked, 'a little
messy'. One of the reasons is certainly that the squalor
of the original story would be much too strong when presented through the realism of the camera. Thus the film,
like the play, draws attention to how utterly dependent
Conrad's tale is on the mode of telling. For instance, the
blowing-up of Stevie in the film was much 'resented' by
the audience; as François Truffaut puts it: 'Making
a child die in a picture is a rather ticklish matter; it comes
close to an abuse of cinematic power.'[6]

NOTES

1. *Ridgway's: A Militant Weekly for God and Country.*
The last number, for 15 December 1906, under the title
'*The Secret Agent:* A Novel Dealing with the Anarchists
of London', continued the serial's chap. 6. It opens with
the passage on p. 204 of the Collected Edition where Heat
realises that the Assistant Commissioner has preceded him
at the Verlocs'. (For further comment on the Assistant
Commissioner's role, see p. 234 below.)

2. Walter F. Wright, *Romance and Tragedy in Joseph
Conrad* (New York, 1949; reprinted 1966) pp. 175–97.

3. See Jocelyn Baines, *Joseph Conrad: A Critical Biography* (London, 1960) pp. 420, 422, 427–8.

4. Walpole, *A Conrad Memorial Library*, p. 169. On the
writing, rehearsal and reception of the play, see Jean-Aubry,

Life and Letters, II 272–83, and R. L. Megroz, *A Talk with Joseph Conrad* (London, 1926). For a contemporary critique of the play, see J. T. Grein, *The New World of the Theatre, 1923–1924* (London, 1924) pp. 1–3. Grein's view that Conrad's play lacked dramatic skill was not shared by Arnold Bennett, who considered it 'certainly the best I have seen for a very, very long time, and by a long way the best' : James Hepburn (ed.), *Letters of Arnold Bennett* (London, 1966) I 317. The dramatic version has been analysed by James Kilroy, 'Conrad's *Succès de Curiosité* : The Dramatic Version of *The Secret Agent*', *English Literature in Transition,* X (1967) 81–8.

5. The credits read : *Production:* Shepherd, Gaumont-British Picture, 1936. *Producers:* Michael Balcon and Ivor Montagu. *Director:* Alfred Hitchcock. *Scenario:* Charles Bennett, from the novel by Joseph Conrad *The Secret Agent. Adaptation:* Alma Reville. *Dialogues:* Ian Hay, Helen Simpson and E. V. H. Emmett. *Director of Photography:* Bernard Knowles. *Sets:* Otto Werndorff and Albert Jullion. *Music:* Louis Levy. *Costumes:* J. Strassner. *Editing:* Charles Frend. *Studio:* Lime Grove. *Cartoon:* Sequence of *Who Killed Cock Robin?* Silly Symphony of Walt Disney, used with his agreement. *Distributors:* G.F.D., 1936, 76 minutes; U.S.A., G.B. Prod., 1937. *Principal Actors:* Sylvia Sidney (Sylvia Verloc), Oscar Homolka (Verloc, her husband), Desmond Tester (Sylvia's brother), John Loder (Ted, the detective), Joyce Barbour (Renée), Matthew Boulton (the Superintendent), and S. J. Barmington, William Dewhurst, Peter a Bull, Torin Thatcher, Austin Trevor, Clare Greet, Sam Wilkinson, Sara Allgood, Martita Hunt, Pamela Bevan.

6. The film is discussed, and there are two pages of stills of the murder scene, in *Hitchcock,* by François Truffaut, with the collaboration of Helen G. Scott (New York, 1967) pp. 75–80.

PART TWO

Critical Essays

John Galsworthy

JOSEPH CONRAD:
A DISQUISITION (1908)

In the composition of a certain plant, chemists have found
a liquid volatile alkaloid, known by the name of nicotine.
Found nowhere else, this essence makes the plant to-
bacco.

And so it is with writers – at least, with great ones. To
the composition of them many qualities and powers contribute, but at the back of all there is secreted something
that differentiates the species.

Now in the writer Joseph Conrad there is present behind his art, and the conscious qualities ranged in service
to express it, a certain cosmic spirit, a power of taking
the reader down below the surface to the earth's heart,
to watch the process that, in its slow, inexorable courses,
has formed a crust, to which are clinging all our little
different living shapes. He has the power of making his
reader feel the inevitable oneness of all things that be,
of breathing into him a sense of solace that he himself is
part of a great unknown Unity.

The irony of things is a nightmare weighing on man's
life, because he has so little of this cosmic spirit; the little
that he has he frequently distrusts, for it seems to him
destructive of the temples that he builds, the gardens he
lays out, the coins he circulates from hand to hand. He
goes in fear of death and of the universe in which he
lives, nor can he bear to think that he is bound up with a
Scheme that seems to him so careless of his own important
life.

The Universe is always saying: The little part called man is smaller than the whole!

Man cannot grasp that statement. He ducks his head resentfully beneath his wing, and hides from contemplation of this truth. It is he who thus creates the irony of things.

Joseph Conrad's writings have the power of persuading man to peep out now and then and see that whole of which he is so small a part. There is no other living English novelist that so reveals the comfort and the beauty of the mystery in which we live, no other that can make us feel how small and stupid, how unsafe and momentary, solution is. If, at the bottom of our hearts, below our network of defences, we did not feel uncertainty, we should expire – suffocated in the swaddling bands of safety – we could not breathe the stagnant air with which we try to fill our houses. It is the essence of this writer to let in the wind with its wild, mysterious savour.

To understand nothing is to love everything. The moment that we really understand, we are no longer curious; but to be curious is to be in love. The man who has the cosmic spirit knows that he will never understand; he spends his life, inquiringly, in love. Nothing is too squalid, too small, too unconventional or remote for him to gaze on and long to know. Joseph Conrad was born in love with knowledge, but he was also born in love with mystery; in a word, he is a lover of the Universe. And so it is that on his canvases the figures he has loved pass and repass across a background that he has loved as much or even more; they step forth and sink back into the great Scheme from which all came and into which we all return. They stand before a backcloth that has not only the dimensions of height and breadth, but that of thickness, a backcloth into which is woven the whole cosmic plan; they live and breathe without detachment, phenomena

f the process which has brought them forth. Epic, often,
n their tragedy and comedy, what makes them epic is the
eeling they inspire, that, for all their firm reality and
detailed, everyday existence, they are shapes embodying
the evolution and the devolution of the spheres. Neither
exalted to the abasement of the Scheme that brought
them forth, nor abased to the exaltation of their author —
they have their just position on the plan of life.

In the novels of Balzac and Charles Dickens there is the
eeling of environment, of the growth of men from men.
n the novels of Turgenev the characters are bathed in
ght; Nature with her many moods is all around, but
nan is first. In the novels of Joseph Conrad, Nature is
rst, man second. The certainty of this is not obtruded
n the reader, it reaches him in subtle ways; it does not
eem conveyed by conscious effort, but through a sort of
emperamental distillation. And it is this feeling for, and
repossession with, the manifestations of mysterious forces
nat gives this writer his unique position among novelists.
he cosmic spirit is not in many men, but in all that have
: there is something of the unethical morality of Nature.
hings, for them, have no beginning and no end. Such
nen stand and watch the plants spring up; watch those
lants growing by the same process that brought them
nto life; watch them in the end returning to the mould
rom which they came. The virtues of this cosmic spirit
re a daring curiosity and courageous resignation; its
alue to the world is in correspondence with its rarity.

If men were not disharmonic, there would be no irony
f things. We jut out everywhere, and fail to see how we
re jutting out. We seek solutions, raise our flags, work
ur arms and legs loyally in the isolated fields that come
within our vision, but, having no feeling for the whole,
he work we do is departmental. The war of the depart-
nents is the game we understand; we spend our lives

keeping up the ball and taking down the score. The rac
of men is a race of partisans feeding their pigeon-hole
with contradictory reports of life, and when a fellow
comes and lays a summary on the desk, they look at hir
askance; but the future pays attention, for the impartia
is all that it has time for.

Art inspired by cosmic spirit is, in fact, the only docu
ment that can be trusted, the only evidence that Tim
does not destroy. Artists are the eyes of that human figur
which symbolises human life, and if this figure is to se
its way at all, its eyes must pierce and be unflinching
Myopia, a cast or squint, a habit of looking on the groun
or at the sky – these sight-defects are dangerous to th
whole body; the things such eyes perceive are not th
things that are; and in the voyage of long discovery tha
man is set on, all shoals not definitely marked, all rock
not accurately seen, all winds not strictly registered, to
gether with the ungauged fluctuations of the man him
self, his tides of temper, his caprices, and his dreads
these are set-backs to the fortune of the voyage.

The just envisagement of things is the first demand w
make of art; it is art's spirit; then comes the manner o
expression, for the quality of art is obviously the qualit
of its technical expression. No man can change the spir
born in him, but daily, hourly, he does change the man
ner of its setting forth. All that he sees and hears, read
writes, and thinks of, even what he dreams, mould an
modify the form of his production. The fuller the trad
tions and life that flood an author's consciousness, th
finer, so long as he keeps his powers, will be the textur
of his output.

This writer, Joseph Conrad, born of families of Polis
gentry who suffered in the rebellion of 1863, sharing a
a child his parents' exile, spending his early manhoo
as a sailor, has laid up a strange store of thought, trad

on, life, and language, and on his manner of production his has stamped itself. As in a fine carpet, with lapse of time, the colours grow more subtle, more austere, so in the carpet of this writer's weaving the bewildering richness of his earlier books is sobered to the clearer, cooler colours of the later. *Almayer's Folly, The Outcast of the Islands, Tales of Unrest* – his first three books – were in a sense surcharged; they gleamed, they were luxuriant, like the tropics where their scenes were laid; they had a certain animal delight in their abundance; they rioted. With *The Nigger of the Narcissus* – that real epic of the sea – the carpet begins to tone; through *Youth* and *Lord Jim* this process of toning is at work, till in *Typhoon* and, above all, in *Falk* a perfect mellowness is reached. *Nostromo*, in some respects his most amazing work, reveals the carpet, as after a visit to the cleaner's, harsher again in colour, somewhat patchy, but *The Mirror of the Sea*, which followed on *Nostromo*, displays it in an evening light, worn to a soberer beauty. As to *The Secret Agent*, our latest glimpse of Joseph Conrad's carpet, the colours are clear and quiet, though we are shown them in a hard, unsparing light.

The writing of these ten books is probably the only writing of the last twelve years that will enrich the English language to any great extent. Other writers will better clarify and mould; this writer, by the native wealth of his imagery, by a more daring and a subtler use of words, brings something new to the fund of English letters. The faults of style are obvious, the merit is the merit of unconscious, and unforced, and, in a sense, of accidental novelty. Style is inseparable from that which expresses, and all that we should fling aside, and rightly, as exotic, if it expressed a futile spirit in new words and images, we instinctively accept with all its flaws when it clothes true insight into life. A language is avid of fresh blood, of all

that ministers to health and stamina; like a human be
ing, it assimilates the cake and rejects the country rock
All that is country rock in Joseph Conrad's writings fall
away; all that is not has passed into the English tongue

Writers of any courage sometimes descend on to the
little earth of creatures they have created, and ask : 'Ar
these persons really living – is it blood, or is it sawdust, i
these veins? I'll try them with a pin!' And with a pi
they go, searching for soft spots, but they never run it in
they are not looking for another's vulnerable spots – an
blood or sawdust that came out would, unfortunately, b
their own. Precious to themselves, they must preserv
the little creatures they have made. So that, though whe
they return to heaven they say : 'This or that one's ver
woodeny!' in their hearts they do not feel them so, for
was they who made them.

But the reader of any courage need not, nor to do hir
justice does he often, spare the bodkin.

On the earth of Joseph Conrad the population teems
and, having tried them with a bodkin, we find very fev
with sawdust in their veins. Some, it is true, such as the
hero in *Lord Jim*, or the husband in the story *The Return*
have been so violently attracted by the man who mad
them that, like true worshippers, they refuse to stan
upon their legs. Intended for stupid men, with the brain
and nerves of such, they will not, out of longing to re
semble their creator, admit that they are stupid. The
pray so to be like him, that their prayer has sometime
been a little heard; they voice too much the thoughts c
their creator. But they are few. Oftener – like Captai
MacWhirr and Mr Jukes in *Typhoon*, and Mr Bake
of *The Nigger*; like the girl in *Falk*; the elderly Frenc
lieutenant in *Lord Jim* : 'a quiet, massive chap in a crease
uniform, sitting drowsily over a tumbler half-full of som
dark liquid'; like the ragged Russian in the *Heart*

Darkness; like Karain the Malay, and Stein the naturalist; like Nostromo's Doctor Monygham; Stevie, Inspector Heat, the Perfect Anarchist, and Mrs Verloc in *The Secret Agent* – they stand up very straight and undismayed, not in the limelight needful to the figures of more fashionable children of the brain; not in the high, dry light of Fielding, Thackeray, or Henry James; not in Turgenev's limpid, sorrowing sunlight; but in a shadowy glamour of their own. Breathing and palpable, clothed firmly in their suitable flesh, they are yet elusive, as though jealous of displaying those dynamic powers which they concrete. They have something of the quality and something of the colouring seen in a Leonardo picture; they quiver with the strength of their vitality; they move amongst black shadows. For Joseph Conrad is an artist who paints in orange, Vandyke-brown, blue, silver, and lamp-black, whose poetry is science, and whose science poetry. And always round these figures, above them, and below, are felt those restless forces, too potent in their restlessness for man, too little potent for the unchanging rhythm that keeps their restlessness controlled.

There is a natural tendency in departmental man, and perhaps especially in Englishmen, to demand of authors that they shall make for our enjoyment so-called 'interesting' characters – not common sailors, anarchists, or outcasts of the islands – but persons of a certain rank and fashion; persons living not in 'sordid squalor', but in gilt-edged certainty; persons not endued with the heroism and the failings of poor human nature, but with gentility; in a word, persons really 'interesting'. This is the great defect of Joseph Conrad's writings. Lamentably lacking in the power of envisaging the world as the private property of a single class, lamentably curious, lamentably sympathetic with all kinds of men, he has failed dismally to produce a single book dealing solely with the upper

classes. All sorts of common people come upon his stage,
and in such a careless way; not that we may laugh at
them, or note the eccentric habits of their kind, but that
we may see them breathing-in their oxygen, loving and
dying, more alive and kicking than the veriest *bourgeois*
of us all. It is a grievous fault! That one who paints a
gentleman as well as Joseph Conrad can, should choose
to paint Verloc, and give us insight, such as few have
given, into a fellow-creature so remarkably deficient in
gentility – this is indeed a waste of force! For, departmental as we are, we feel we only want to know the things
that help us to be departmental. Before the departmental
man there shines a climbing star. The stars that he who
has the cosmic spirit sees are stars that never climb; fixed
as fate, they throw their rays.

But there is one faculty of Joseph Conrad's writings
for which even departmental Britons may be grateful
It is his kindly diagnosis of the departmental Briton. Pri-
soners in the cells of our own nationality, we never see
ourselves; it is reserved for one outside looking through
the tell-tale peep-hole to get a proper view of us. So much
the better when the eye that peeps is loving! In the whole
range of his discovery there is no man that better pleases
Joseph Conrad than this same departmental Briton, man
of action, man of simple faith, man unvisited by hesitation – in sum, the man of enterprise, with all his qualities
and limitations. He has painted this type a dozen times
– Captains Lingard, Allison, MacWhirr, Mr Baker, Mr
Jukes, Mr Creighton, Inspector Heat, and many more

Detached by temperament and blood, this writer sees
that sort of Briton with a tender irony that brings out all
his foibles, but also an essential sturdiness of soul which
makes him one to have beside you on a dark and windy
night. Seeing him objectively and without confusion,
knowing him personally in all those hours that test the

emper of the heart, and having felt his value at first and, Joseph Conrad has hung on our too-little grateful walls the most seizing portraits of the man of action that our literature can show. For evidence as poignant of this type we have to go to Speke's delicious, naïve presentment of himself in his journal of the Nile's discovery. We learn, subjectively, from that what Speke had no desire to tell, no interest in telling, no power of seeing when the tale was old; we learn, reading between the lines, with our tongues pressed against our cheeks, what a force is 'no imagination'; we learn, too, with our tongues restored, the meaning of the word 'indomitable'. But to learn from Speke's unconscious revelation we must have our wits about us and construct his figure for ourselves; to learn from Joseph Conrad's object-pictures we need only eyes.

Side by side with these impervious spirits he has been through all the peril of the sea, watching to see how they would take it, and he has found they took it very well. So there has grown up in his heart a laughing admiration, a sense of safety and reliance on a kind of man who really would be frightened if he could; and with that laughing admiration he has set him down, not once, but many times.

In the features of those truthful portraits one seems to read the kindly artist's verdict : 'On a lee shore, sirs, there are worse things than "no imagination" !'

There hang the pictures if we had eyes !

Eyes; it seems a little thing ! But to 'see' is the greatest gift of all. The surface of the world is open enough to everybody's gaze; that which lies behind the surface is what lies in the gazer's soul, the beauty which everyday phenomena evoke out of the seer's consciousness. Everything is beautiful to those who have the humour to perceive. Birth and decay, virtue and vice, youth and old age, even the real and touching value of the departmental

Briton – all these the seer Joseph Conrad sees, and ha
put in terms of a profound philosophy.

SOURCE: *Fortnightly Review*, no. 496 (1 April 1908
pp. 627-33

Thomas Mann

JOSEPH CONRAD'S
THE SECRET AGENT (1926)

Once before I have had occasion to write of a case like
the present one: when I contributed a preface to an
edition of *Peter Schlemil*, the happiest creation of a German writer of French nationality, and one of the best
prized and loved of German literary possessions. And
here, in this Polish Englishman, we have the modern
pendant to Chamisso, only that this time we are trans-
lators only, it is not our national charms that are being
flattered! Yet that should not lessen our pleasure in the
rare and beautiful phenomenon; rather we should yield
to its spell with enjoyment unmixed with envy – just as
once others looked upon the phenomenon of Chamisso's
German authorship. Cases of individuals of one nation
falling in love with the life forms of another one; of deliberate and definite emigration, complete personal and
intellectual naturalisation into another sphere, as though
nature had made a mistake and human intelligence had
corrected it – such cases, it would seem, recur with a certain regularity in the history of culture, in the history of
literature. And those whose healthy reverence for the
natural is mingled with some little ironic doubt – probably
less healthy but, humanly speaking, not without dignity
– on the score of that undubitably holy element, will not
be moved to sneer at the phenomenon as a monstrosity.
On the contrary, they will note with sympathy and satisfaction a case of freedom from national limitations which

did not issue in formlessness and mental death but in a universally admired cultural achievement.

It would be hard to say on what grounds to-day a Frenchman would make Germany his spiritual home. Once, in a more romantic time, it could happen out of love of poetry. We were the land of poets and thinkers; to be a poet and to write German verse were, up to a point, one and the same thing. Who felt drawn to poesy felt drawn to Germany – Chamisso became German in order to be a German poet. But Conrad's case is different in kind; not only the nations are different but also the times have changed. The Pole certainly did not become English in order to be an English writer. So far as I can learn, the idea was far from him. He became English to be a sailor – out of irresistible love of the sea. And here the two cases display likeness again : to be a sailor, Conrad might have become 'a Russian, a Frenchman or a Prussian', he might have entered any of these marines, and thus it must have been that England and seafaring fell together, in the same way as once Germany and poetry to the author of *Peter Schlemil*. In both cases we have a shift of nationality caused by a passion for the main preoccupation of another people, the calling in which that one proverbially shines in the others' eyes. It was an accident of the time that Conrad's motive was in its nature less intellectual than Chamisso's.

But, after all, it would be rather old-fashioned and romantic to define the intellectual so narrowly as to make is synonymous with the literary. The Pole's love of the sea, which to him was the English thing, must always have been bound up with a deep sympathy for the essentially English, the English temperament and attitude toward life, the English accent and the spirit of its language; such a passion is not possible to conceive without intellectual and speech elements. At bottom Conrad's conversion was scarcely less 'poetic' than Chamisso's. And – after becoming an English sailor – he would scarcely have become an English author, had not creation been a primal impulse of his being; if his whole strange course, away from all natural ties and into a foreign sphere of his own mysterious election, had not already been that of a dreamer and poet.

His love of the sea, of adventures at sea, was certainly a poet-love; of her, of life upon her and with her, of that almost alone, he has written, even after he left her for the solid ground; written in English, the classical tongue of the seafaring man – such English that, to a foreigner at least, it seems it could hardly be more so, and that to-day his European reputation is that of a great British author.

When some years ago I visited The Hague, John Galsworthy was lecturing there on 'Conrad and Tolstoy'. Who it was, whom Galsworthy was setting beside the Russian colossus, I had no notion; and my amazement increased when I heard that André Gide had learned English in order to read Conrad in the original. Since that time I have read some of the best works by this narrative genius : the dæmonic story of a storm, called *The Nigger of the Narcissus*, and that of a calm, called *The Shadow Line*, also some of those whose scene is laid partly or wholly on shore, like *Chance*, a performance of great technical intricacy and brilliant virtuosity, and the altogether thrilling 'crime story', *The Secret Agent*. I have read enough to feel it laid upon me to give something of him to the German public, whether maritime or not – and perhaps not maritime, perhaps just this very admirable *Secret Agent*, for the reason that it would be a limitation of Conrad's fame to speak of him only as a writer of sea-tales. I agree that this man's very deepest and most personal experience has been the sea, his perilous fellowship

with that mighty element; certainly his greatest creative
achievements lie in this field. But his virile talent, his
Englishness, his free brow, his clear, steady and humorous
eye, his narrative verve, power and grave-faced whim
sicality, show up as well when the author stops on dry
ground and observes what goes on there; sees it, sees
through it and gives it form and body, as in the story
lying before me, this exciting, yes, thrilling tale, a 'crime
story', as I said, and a political novel to boot, the history
of a foreign embassy intrigue and its tragic human out
come.

It is an anti-Russian story, plainly enough, anti
Russian in a very British sense and spirit. Its background
consists in politics on the large scale, in the whole conflict
between the British and the Russian political ideology
I think it possible that this conflict has always formed the
background – I will not say the motive – of the Pole's
passionate love of England. If I were dealing with a Ger
man the hypothesis would be a doubtful one. We are
metaphysicians; neither consciously nor unconsciously
would we ever yield the political that much influence
upon our mental life. But we have begun to feel that per
haps other people are different; and that feeling is the
source of my guess that Polish Russophobia is here ex
pressing itself in British.

And particularly in the figure of Mr Vladimir, secre
tary to the representative of a foreign, all too foreign
power in London. The guilt of the whole affair lies at his
door. He is a man of considerable elegance, though the
author seems to agree with the verdict of one of the char
acters who calls him a 'hyperborean swine'. Of polished
manners in general, he betrays in emotion a 'somewhat
oriental phraseology' and a guttural accent that is not
only un-English but un-European, even Central Asiatic
'Descended from generations victimised by the instru

nents of arbitrary power,' it says of him, 'he was racially, nationally and individually afraid of the police. He was born to it. But that sentiment, which resembled the unnatural horror some people have of cats, did not stand in the way of his immense contempt for the English police.' 'The vigilance of the police,' says he, or one of his subordinates says it for him, 'and the severity of the magistrates! The general leniency of the judicial procedure here, and the utter absence of all repressive measures, are a scandal to Europe. What is wished for just now is the accentuation of the unrest – of the fermentation which undoubtedly exists.' An international conference, that is, is to be held in Milan to combat social revolution. 'What we want is to administer a tonic to the conference in Milan,' he said airily. 'Its deliberations upon international action for the suppression of political crime don't seem to get anywhere. England lags. This country is absurd with its sentimental regard for individual liberty. . . England must be brought into line.'

This anti-Sarmatic[1] satire, however light the touch, speaks pride of English freedom and English civilisation in every line. Hated Russia, hated now in British but perhaps originally in Polish, is made to bear the guilt of all the human tragedy which is the matter of the novel: the death of little Stevie, the murder of the pitiable rascal Verloc and the suicide of his wife. Is Conrad more English in any of his shipboard tales than in this political detective story? An upright British Police Commissioner says to Mr Vladimir: 'What pleased me most in this affair, is that it makes such an excellent starting-point for a piece of work which I've felt must be taken in hand – that is, the clearing out of this country of all the foreign political spies, police, and that sort of – of – dogs.' 'Dogs' is an expression of Mr Vladimir, an Oriental, Central Asian sort of expression, to speak in that singular

guttural tone which the Soviet agents of to-day probably
command quite as well as did persons of Mr Vladimir's
kidney. I mention this only to show that our novel is not
out of date because its action takes place under the Czars
and that the conflict of West and East which forms its
political background has lost nothing in timeliness by a
change of government.

And here another guess: the unequivocal, the ever
tendentious Western bias of this extraordinary writer
who has for years been famous in England, France and
America – might it not perhaps be responsible for the
limited scope of his reputation in a country like ours,
which must always instinctively shrink from casting a de-
cisive vote on one side or the other? There was a time
when it looked as though we had chosen, as though we
had voted, politically and culturally, on the side of the
East; and that was just the time when Conrad's name
was becoming celebrated throughout the Western world.
For us the possessor of this narrative gift stands in the
shadow of Dostoevsky – a shadow which, we are free to
confess, even to-day, we feel could swallow up three or
four Conrads. And yet time changes all things; that epi-
leptic, apocalyptic visionary has to a certain extent lost
his power over the German mind; we are groping our
way back from the Byzantine-Christian East to the
Centre, and so to that in us which is of the humanistic
and liberal West. Probably the very fact that a leading
publisher is now getting out a German edition of Conrad's chief works is evidence of his better chances of success among us.

No, Conrad is far from being the size of Dostoevsky.
But is it size alone that conditions our love? If so, then
our present epoch, which so far has produced forms much
more slender and inconsiderable than those of the nineteenth century, would have small claims on our affec-

ions – and we have already pronounced on the latter as
reat indeed, though most unhappy. Let us confess that
he products of our own century, so much less heroic than
hose of the nineteenth, do not even excel them in refinement. In Wagner, in Dostoevsky, even in Bismarck, the
nineteenth century combines a giant growth with the ex-
reme of subtlety, with a refinement of technique which
ven borders on the morbid and the barbaric. But perhaps
he very abandonment of this characteristic, at once sickly
nd savage, an Asiatic element, one might almost say,
as actually conditioned the smaller structure of our own
me. At least we do find it a more congenial and brotherly
poch, by contrast with the paternalistic spirit of yester-
ay. Perhaps our more modest scale is due to our aspira-
ions toward a purer, brighter, healthier, almost might
ne say a more Greek humanity than the monumental
loom of the nineteenth century knew. And the Anglo-
nania of Conrad the Slav, his scorn of Central Asian
utturals, may be rooted in these very aspirations – or
his very task – of ours.

I would not forget the world-revolution, nor the spiri-
ual advantages that to-day are bound up with good rela-
ons with the East. Every open-eyed Westerner today
nvies the Central European on purely geographical
rounds, for advantages which would doubtless have to
e surrendered in going over completely to the bourgeois
West. In a sense we should have to reckon with a penalty
even without conceding that English against Conti-
ental European means in itself a lowering of the level.
More form, with more limitations – was that the alter-
ative the Slav faced when he made his choice? No,
hat puts it badly. What he gave up were the advantages
f barbarism, which he did open-eyed. What he got was
eason, moderation, the open-minded attitude, intellec-
ual freedom, and a humour that is saved by its Anglo-

Saxon robustness from falling into the sentimental and
bourgeois. A crisp, breezy humour it is, animated to some
extent by the sentiment expressed somewhere in *Th*
Secret Agent, that 'this world of ours is not such a ver
serious affair after all'. He shows small memory of the
reverence for suffering that is a feature of Eastern Chris
tianity; when he speaks of the hook which a poor ol
coachman has sticking out his sleeve instead of an arm
he does so with a dryness that expresses grim enjoymen
of life rather than a sense of pity. Often, in unobtrusiv
details, this humour is refreshingly comic: as when h
describes the cab drive and the glass of the near-by hous
fronts rattling and jingling as though about to collaps
behind the cab; or the mechanical piano, whose key
seem to be played on by a vulgar and impudent ghos
who breaks off as though gone grumpy. The author doe
not, even faintly, change his key in describing a murdere
man: 'Mr Verloc did not seem so much asleep now a
lying down with a bent head and looking intently at h
left breast. And when Comrade Ossipon had made ou
the handle of the knife he turned away from the glaze
door and retched violently.' Here all ado is lacking. Th
gaze turned upon the horrible is clear, lively, dry-eyed
almost gratified; the spirit of the narration is impressivel
English, and at the same time it is ultra-modern, pos
middle-class. For I feel that, broadly and essentially, th
striking feature of modern art is that it has ceased to re
cognise the categories of tragic and comic, or the dramati
classifications, tragedy and comedy. It sees life as trag
comedy, with the result that the grotesque is its mos
genuine style – to the extent, indeed, that to-day that is th
only guise in which the sublime may appear. For, if
may say so, the grotesque is the genuine anti-bourgeo
style; and however bourgeois Anglo-Saxondom ma
otherwise be or appear, it is a fact that in art the comi

grotesque has always been its strong point.

No, Conrad's leaning to the West is not an indication of artistic or intellectual surrender to the bourgeois point of view. He puts into Mr Vladimir's mouth a question full of social and critical implications when he makes him ask: 'I suppose you agree that the middle-classes are stupid?' and when Mr Verloc replies 'They are', we have no doubt that the author shares the opinion of the two men. Conrad is too much artist and free spirit to be doctrinaire in his socialism – or to be Socialist at all save in the freest sense and as a child of his time. Marxism is represented in the book by the monomania of the solitary Michaelis, the 'ticket-of-leave apostle'. Conrad's revolutionaries are hardly lovable types; the psychology of his social rebels is strongly pessimistic in kind; and his scepticism of social utopias is revealed in the description of one insurgent of 'an immense and nice hospital with a garden of flowers, in which the strong are to devote themselves to the nursing of the weak', whereas another, a miserable little terrorist and professor of dynamiting, dreams of quite another kind, a world like a slaughterhouse, whither the 'weak' are carried to be extinguished. But all this sarcasm is hardly bourgeois in intention. It is very pretty irony to say of the good Mr Verloc that his function was to protect society, not to improve it or pass judgment upon it; the irony becomes great satire when it deals with the main action of the book, the dynamite outrage which is to stimulate the Milan conference, and with the object upon which it would be most profitably directed.

'Of course, there is art. A bomb in the National Gallery would make some noise. But it would not be serious enough. Art has never been the fetish of the middle-class. It's like breaking a few back windows in a man's house;

whereas if you want to make him really sit up, you must try at least to raise the roof. There would be some screaming, of course, but from whom? Artists – art critics and such like, people of no account. . . . But there is learning – science. Any imbecile that has got an income believes in that. He does not know why, but he believes it matters somehow. It is the sacrosanct fetish. . . . It will alarm every selfishness of the class which should be impressed. They believe that in some mysterious way science is at the source of their material prosperity. They do. . . . Murder is always with us. It is almost an institution. The demonstration must be against learning – science. . . . What do you think of having a go at astronomy? . . . There could be nothing better. . . . The whole civilised world has heard of Greenwich. The very bootblacks in the basement of Charing Cross station know something of it. See? . . . Go for the first meridian. You don't know the middle-classes as well as I do. Their sensibilities are jaded. The first meridian. Nothing better, and nothing easier, I should think.'

These judicious instructions of Mr Vladimir to poor Verloc are the satirical height of the book. Its author is not, of course, the kind of creature who despises science. Nor, on the other hand, would he care much for a society based wholly upon it and throbbing to its dicta; and he speaks of 'that glance of insufferable, hopelessly dense sufficiency which nothing but the frequentation of science can give to the dullness of common mortals'. Disregard for art, for what constitutes the things of the mind, combined with boundless credulity and reverence for utilitarian science – that Conrad feels to be bourgeois. If his attitude toward the proletariat is not quite orthodox, that is obviously because science, on the other side of Marxism, has become the heritage and fetish of the proletariat; nobody will deny that Bolshevism is a sternly scientific conception of the world.

Comrade Ossipon, for instance – nicknamed 'Doctor'; sometime medical practitioner without diploma, peripatetic lecturer to labour unions on the social future of hygiene, author of a confiscated pamphlet on 'The Corroding Vices of the Middle Classes' – Comrade Ossipon is scientific. 'Typical of this form of degeneracy' is what he says, condescendingly, of little Stevie's circle-drawing, that singular occupation, practised with so much assiduity, a cosmic chaos as it were, or the efforts of an insane art to portray the inconceivable. Of course Comrade Ossipon refers to the ear-lobes and to Lombroso. And 'Lombroso is an ass', answers him a still greater enemy of the existing order; and the author characterises this as a 'shattering blasphemy'.

'Did you ever see such an idiot? For him the criminal is the prisoner. Simple, is it not? What about those who shut him up there – forced him in there? . . . And what is crime? Does he know that, this imbecile who has made his way in this world of gorged fools by looking at the ears and teeth of a lot of poor, luckless devils? Teeth and ears mark the criminal? Do they? And what about the law that marks him still better – the pretty branding iron invented by the overfed to protect themselves against the hungry? Red-hot applications on their vile skins, hey? Can't you smell and hear from here the thick hide of the people burn and sizzle? That's how criminals are made for your Lombrosos to write their silly stuff about.'

With all this 'blasphemy' the author probably feels a certain, perhaps considerable, degree of sympathy. But his own way of looking at and describing little Stevie shows that his objections to Lombroso's science – as a cheapish middle-class product – rest not upon social grounds, but upon profounder, religious ones.

Stevie, as revealed during the cab-drive and the ensuing

conversation with his sister Winnie, in so far as his 'peculiarity' permits one to speak of conversation; this deficient little Stevie, who nevertheless is lovable above and beyond all values in life, and whom Winnie so loves that she avenges his death in the most frightful, self-immolating manner – Stevie is far and away the finest figure in the book, and conceived with the liveliest and most affecting sympathy. Here Russian influence is plain: without Dostoevsky's Idiot Stevie is unthinkable; we must admit that Dostoevsky's attempt to present the purest and holiest in our humanity on a basis of the patho-logical is incomparably greater in its scope; yet here too we have an effort to canonise the clinically deficient. Our author's very modern power of seeing both sides is shown in his never belittling the pathological side of the case or romantically closing his eyes to it. He makes a naturalistic concession to science by characterising Stevie's 'peculiar-ity' as a family trait; and gives pathological significance to his sister's deed by mentioning the sudden and striking likeness she shows with her brother at the moment of it. None the less, the dominant psychology here is one with a religious implication which shows Comrade Ossipon's 'scientific' opinion of Stevie for what, from the human point of view, it really is: a shabby pseudo-education. Indeed, there is a subtle yet unmistakable suggestion that Comrade Ossipon's remark is what drops into the harassed mind of Verloc the first germ of the idea that he might use Stevie in the political crime he meditates; thus science is once more compromised, once more found guilty from the human point of view.

All which is not bourgeois, but neither is it good ortho-dox proletarianism. It is evidence of the untrammelled objectivity which is the business of the class-free writer – if perhaps only his; and everywhere in Conrad's books it is displayed at its liberating task. In his judgment of the sexes he is objective: speaks of the sensitivity that can exist in the masculine nature alongside exasperating brutality; and finds that women are naturally more artful than men and much more ruthlessly avid for detail. So also he is aloof and critical in his attitude toward classes and masses, to all the apparent and temporary contradictions in the world. The sarcasm he directs against 'hygienic idleness' as a form of existence is quite good socialism; but he also knows how to make repulsive to the soul of the reader the type of the hoarse-voiced agitator – as in *The Nigger of the Narcissus*; and he says of his terrorists that they are not a hair better than the powers invoked against them. 'Like to like. The terrorists and the policemen both come from the same basket. Revolution, legality – counter moves in the same game.' That is not the idle indifference of a detached observer. It is the refusal of a very much engaged intelligence to hang miserably in the air between contraries. 'You revolutionists', he says, or makes someone say, 'are the slaves of the social convention, which is afraid of you; slaves of it as much as the very police that stand up in defence of that convention. Clearly you are, since you want to revolutionise it. It governs your thoughts, of course, and your action too, and thus neither your thought nor your action can ever be conclusive.'

Conrad's objectivity may seem cool; but is a passion – a passion for freedom. It is the expression of the very same love and passion that drove the young Pole to sea; and that – as once in the case of Ivan Turgenev – was doubtless the profoundest motive of his cultural relations with the West. This love of freedom cannot be confused with bourgeois liberalism, for he is an artist; and it is far too robust to be classed as aestheticism. The extent of Conrad's artistic success in Germany will be measured by his talent. His intellectual message will be for those among us who believe – in opposition to the views of the large majority – that the idea of freedom has a rôle to play in Europe that is not yet played out.

SOURCE: *Past Masters, and Other Papers* (1933) pp. 231–47; the essay originally appeared as the preface to a German translation (*Der Geheimagent*, 1926) of *The Secret Agent*.

NOTE

1. From Sarmatia, a district in Southern Russia on the Don. [Ed.]

Hugh Walpole

FROM
A CONRAD MEMORIAL LIBRARY
(1929)

Among the many comments, critical and otherwise, on Conrad's works since his death, there have been far too few, in my opinion, on the simple and narrative side of his genius. I say simple because in these after-war days when the novel is made either a philosophical treatise or a rag-bag of personal reactions to daily living, the art of narrative *does* seem simple, simple-minded, that is. And here I would earnestly remark that it is only a prejudiced and child-like criticism that will scorn the modern analytical novel when it is finely done. The modern novel is enriched by the voyages of *Ulysses* and the thrilling discoveries of Marcel Proust, but when is someone going to recognize that the art of external narrative is waiting desperately for the genius who will give us the modern equivalent of Scott and Dumas just as Joyce and Proust have given us the modern equivalent of Richardson and Sterne – yes, and on the same grand scale?

Conrad would have laughed, shrugged his shoulders, and it might be, raged, had you suggested to him anything so portentous. He rejected again and again the notion that he was 'out' for any ism. But his constant reiteration that everything about him was 'simple' – his art, his philosophy of life, his sense of adventure, his comprehension of danger and struggle – has always been to myself a little suspect.

How can he, for instance, after the ghastly struggle that is revealed to us in his letters to Edward Garnett over *The Rescue*, have supposed in his heart that anything in *that* was simple? Knowing him, nothing about him appeared to be simple, save his courtesy, no, not even his gout. Finance was not to him simple, nor domesticity, nor paternity, nor friendship (since that last involved for him so many more things than it involved apparently for most people).

No, in spite of all the letters, the books, the lives and the summaries, the truth about Conrad the man has not yet begun to be told — and perhaps never will be.

But it is not about Conrad the man that I am writing here, but Conrad the story-teller. That and nothing more. He began to write in England when *good* story-telling in *good* English was still the fashion. Stevenson's shadow hung over the scene and there were Quiller-Couch, Stanley Weyman, Marriott Watson and many another, all trying to make an art of narrative, and some of them succeeding.

It wasn't then a thing of which anyone need be ashamed that he could tell a good story, and it is a fact upon which I make no comment that it is the stories rather than the psychological experiments that have survived from the early nineties. Wells's *War of the Worlds*, Q's *Splendid Spur*, Weyman's *Gentleman of France*, Haggard's *She*, Hope's *Prisoner of Zenda*.

It is very largely due to Conrad that such very simple — but alive — narratives as these can never again be written in English. He took them and added something to them — and what he added was — human beings. Those old stories are alive still to-day because the narrative work in them was so good. But who can pretend that there is among them all a single living, breathing character who exists for us after the book is closed? Not Weyman's

melancholy and elderly hero, nor Q's bold boy and girl,
nor Haggard's honest Quatermain, nor Hope's gentle-
manly but very stupid Rassendyl.

Conrad blazed the way for the newer novelists, and
it isn't his fault if among the many interesting paths that
they have followed they have almost completely neglected
his own brilliant new country.

Alone among historical novelists Walter Scott had
shown it before him, and there are more links between
Old Mortality and *Chance*, between *The Bride of Lam-
mermoor* and *The Arrow of Gold* than anyone has apparently cared to examine. But a novel like *The Secret Agent*
gives us exactly the position.

Here in its barest essentials is a story for Mr A. E. W.
Mason or at a rather simpler degree, Mr Phillips
Oppenheim – a story of plot, political intrigue, bomb-
throwing, secret police, and murder. And out of this plot
rises Verloc looking 'as though he had wallowed all night
on an unmade bed'.[1]

The incidents are, if you examine them, nude, so to
speak, compact of melodrama. What is melodrama? It
is the taking of an abnormal incident and falsely persuading the reader that it is not abnormal. The drama, on the
other hand, consists in taking a very ordinary incident
and persuading a hitherto unobservant watcher that it
is dramatic.

Bombs and murder are, in England at any rate, abnormal incidents, but Conrad does not fall to melodrama,
because he does not pretend that these incidents are normal – he concentrates our attention on the normal people
who take part in them, and as soon as he concentrates
on the people rather than the incidents he enlarges the
whole school of romantic adventure.

Verloc, Winnie Verloc, the idiot boy *might* have been
concerned in the theft of six postage stamps from a pillar-

box in Brixton and would have enabled Conrad to give us all his creative gifts in the making of them just as easily. But implicating them in abnormal events he redoubles his dramatic values because he shows us that human nature does not change one jot, place it in any situation that you please.

The reader, therefore, is permitted a legitimate excitement in the narrative (because, human nature entirely apart, throwing a bomb *is* more exciting than stealing a bottle of beer) but he is never threatened with the nullification of character that most 'stories' written as 'stories' seem to insist upon.

We are told a striking story about the Verlocs, but their vitality does not at all depend on the story. Conrad could have chosen a thousand stories about the Verlocs and they all would have been interesting because the Verlocs are interesting. Divorce Porthos, Athos, and Aramis from their physical movements and what are they? But Conrad allows you to pay your money and have your fun in two different directions.

Incidentally, the most striking thing in this book is not the throwing of the bomb but the ride in the cab. I am inclined to consider that ride in the cab the most beautiful, touching, and moving thing in the whole of Conrad – in any case it is one of the great things in English literature. And the greatness of it does not come alone from characters, but also from events.

Had Conrad not been a master of narrative, had he not chosen to tell stories in his books, but to deal only in psychological aesthetics, then we should have still believed in Verloc and Winnie and the boy. We should still have cared what they did next, but we should not have had the extra fun of watching the excitement of event rising out of event.

His unfinished novel *Suspense* – surely a magnificent

fragment – leaves us with the most eager curiosity about the minds and souls of that extraordinary group of characters, but it leaves us also, like children, with our mouths open, wondering whether Napoleon appeared on the scene, whither floated the intrepid hero, and so on. Surely this is a legitimate interest and an interest to-day far too readily neglected by our modern intellectual novelists. Or is it that the narrative art is too difficult for them, or rather not so much the narrative gift as the going of it hand-in-hand with the creation of character?

At any rate no one at present shows any signs of carrying Conrad's experiments further.

SOURCE : *A Conrad Memorial Library: The Collection of George T. Keating* (1929) pp. 159–63.

NOTE

1. [Editor's Note.] In one of the first editions of *The Secret Agent* in the collection of George T. Keating, Hugh Walpole wrote : 'This has always been to myself one of the most fascinating of Conrad's works because in it and especially in Verloc one discerns a side of Conrad that the sea helped him to disguise. I remember that he once said to me that he fancied that Verloc and Mr Jones of *Victory* were signs of what he might have done in letters had the sea not swept over him. He meant – his sense of evil in the human heart. He clung on to his sea captains because they were his answer to the Verlocs, but I fancy that the Verlocs were always more real to him than the MacWhirrs. Always when I read this book I see myself on a summer day sitting with Lawrence of Arabian fame in Conrad's garden at Bishopsbourne, and Conrad stepping across the grass to us and saying : 'Verloc's just left' and, turning, I saw a fat, humped figure going out of the gates – some journalist from Canterbury.'

F. R. Leavis

FROM
THE GREAT TRADITION (1948)

The Secret Agent . . . is . . . indubitably a classic and a masterpiece, and it doesn't answer to the notion at all – which is perhaps why it appears to have had nothing like due recognition. If we call it an ironic novel, it is with the same intention of the adjective as when *Jonathan Wild* is called an ironic novel. To note this is to be reminded, with a fresh shock, of the inertia of conventional valuation that makes *Jonathan Wild* a masterpiece and the classic of its *genre*. For *The Secret Agent* is truly classical in its maturity of attitude and the consummateness of the art in which this finds expression; in the contrast there is nothing for it but to see *Jonathan Wild* as the clumsy piece of hobbledehoydom, artistic and intellectual, that it is. The irony of *The Secret Agent* is not a matter of an insistent and obvious 'significance' of tone, or the endless repetition of a simple formula. The tone is truly subtle – subtle with the subtlety of the theme; and the theme develops itself in a complex organic structure. The effect depends upon an interplay of contrasting moral perspectives, and the rich economy of the pattern they make relates *The Secret Agent* to *Nostromo*: the two works, for all the great differences between them in range and temper, are triumphs of the same art – the aim of *The Secret Agent*, of course, confines the range, and the kind of irony involves a limiting detachment (we don't look for the secrets of Conrad's soul in *The Secret Agent*).

The matter, the 'story', is that of a thriller – terrorist conclaves, embassy machinations, bomb-outrage, detection, murder, suicide; and to make, in treating such matter with all the refinements of his craft, a sophisticated moral interest the controlling principle is, we recognize, characteristic Conrad. His irony bears on the egocentric naïveties of moral conviction, the conventionality of conventional moral attitudes, and the obtuse assurance with which habit and self-interest assert absolute rights and wrongs. The pattern of the book is contrived to make us feel the different actors or lives as insulated currents of feeling and purpose – insulated, but committed to co-existence and interaction in what they don't question to be a common world, and sometimes making disconcerting contacts through the insulation.

The Verlocs, husband and wife, take their mutual insulation so for granted as to be mainly unconscious of it. What Mr Verloc is becomes plain to us very early on. We see him leaving behind him the shop, fly-staled and dusty, with its display of revolutionary literature and pornographic goods, and making his way westward towards the Embassy of a Foreign Power. Conrad's London bears something of the same kind of relation to Dickens as Henry James's does in *The Princess Casamassima*. The direct influence of Dickens is unmistakable in certain minor lapses into facetious humour (see, for instance, in the account of Verloc's walk, the bit about No. 1 Chesham Square) from the characteristic astringent dryness. There is also, later, a major instance of obvious and unfortunate indebtedness to Dickens in the fantastic slow-motion macabre of the cab-journey to the almshouse. But *The Secret Agent* (unlike *The Princess Casamassima*) is one of the author's most successful works; its strength is something so utterly outside Dickens's compass as to have enabled Conrad to be influenced by him to purely

Conradian ends. And the essential relation to Dickens, it should be plain, is not a matter of being influenced for good or ill, but lies in that energy of vision and characterization which, we have seen, is sometimes as apt to make us say 'Shakespearean' as 'Dickensian'.

We have it in the interview between Verloc and Mr Vladimir, First Secretary of the Embassy. The dialogue – and this is so throughout the book, for all the uncertainty about points of English usage apparent on practically every page of Conrad to the end – is consummate in its blend of inevitable naturalness with strict economy of relevance, and the whole is so dramatically realized that we are hardly aware of shifts to description, stage directions or reported thought: it all seems to be enacted before us.

In the pause Mr Vladimir formulated in his mind a series of disparaging remarks concerning Mr Verloc's face and figure. The fellow was unexpectedly vulgar, heavy and impudently unintelligent. He looked uncommonly like a master plumber come to present his bill. The first Secretary of the Embassy, from his occasional excursions into the field of American humour, had formed a special notion of that class of mechanic as the embodiment of fraudulent laziness and incompetency.

Mr Vladimir himself we see with a vision heightened by Verloc's consternation and disgust:

This anger was complicated by incredulity. And suddenly it dawned upon him that all was an elaborate joke. Mr Vladimir exhibited his white teeth in a smile, with dimples on his round, full face posed with a complacent inclination above the bristling bow of his neck-tie. The favourite of intelligent society women had assumed his drawing-room attitude accompanying the delivery of delicate witticisms. Sitting well forward, his white hand upraised, he seemed to hold delicately between his thumb and forefinger the subtlety of his suggestion.

What he has enjoined upon Verloc, not as a joke but seriously, as a means of waking up the English police to a sense of their European responsibilities, is a bomb-attack upon Greenwich Observatory. Verloc, threatened in his routine comfort and indolence, feels not only helpless anger but a sense of moral outrage too :

'It will cost money,' Mr Verloc said, by a sort of instinct.
'That cock won't fight,' Mr Vladimir retorted, with an amazingly genuine English accent. 'You'll get your screw every month, and no more till something happens. And if nothing happens very soon you won't get even that. What's your ostensible occupation? What are you supposed to live by?'
'I keep a shop,' answered Mr Verloc.
'A shop ! What sort of shop?'
'Stationery, newspapers. My wife –'
'Your what?' interrupted Mr Vladimir in his guttural Central Asian tones.
'My wife,' Mr Verloc raised his husky voice slightly. 'I am married.'
'That be damned for a yarn,' exclaimed the other in unfeigned astonishment. 'Married ! And you a professed anarchist, too ! What is this confounded nonsense? But I suppose it's merely a matter of speaking. Anarchists don't marry. It's well known. They can't. It would be apostasy.'

Actually Verloc is most respectably married. It is a triumph of the irony that we not only see him as a sympathetic character compared with Mr Vladimir, but find ourselves on the point of saying that he is in all essentials an ordinary respectable citizen, concerned like any other to maintain himself and his wife in security and comfort :

the shop, with its squalid trade and anarchistic frequentation, and the complicated treacheries of his profession, we see with him as matters of habit and routine, means to the end. In the final scene with his wife, when he tries to make her understand the full enormity of Mr Vladimir's conduct, he says with righteous exasperation and with all the unction of an outraged moral sense :

'There isn't a murdering plot for the last eleven years that I haven't had my finger in at the risk of my life. There's scores of these revolutionaries I've sent off, with their bombs in their blamed pockets, to get themselves caught on the frontier. The old Baron knew what I was worth to his country. And here suddenly a swine comes along – an ignorant, overbearing swine.'

What Mrs Verloc is comes out only bit by bit – the perfection of the structure of the book shows itself notably in the way in which we are put in possession of the necessary knowledge about her at the right time. We see her serving in the shop with intimidating aplomb, taking the frequentations of the revolutionists as a matter of course, and, placid good wife to a good husband, being tactfully solicitous about his health and comfort. His business, she knows, entails these and other associates, late absences from home, and occasional trips to the Continent; further, she doesn't inquire :

Mrs Verloc wasted no portion of this transient life in seeking for fundamental information. This is a sort of economy having all the appearances and some of the advantages of prudence. Obviously it may be good for one not to know too much. And such a view accords very well with constitutional indolence.

Her mother, who lives with them, and who isn't given
to asking questions either, sometimes wonders why Winnie, an attractive girl, married Mr Verloc. It was, as a
matter of fact, for the very reason that leads the mother
to withdraw to an almshouse, there to spend in loneliness
the remainder of his life : concern for the future of Stevie,
the half-witted younger brother. One of the most poignant
touches of irony in the book is when Winnie says : 'That
poor boy will miss you something cruel. I wish you had
thought a little of that, mother.'

They had both, as a matter of fact, sacrificed themselves for Stevie. And Winnie now, with concealed
anxiety, sets to work to impress Verloc with Stevie's devotion to him. Verloc is lost in the obsessing dreads and
perplexities associated with the face of Mr Vladimir;
but, with Stevie's existence thus forced on his notice, he
realizes Stevie's useful potentialities and is inspired with
a timely idea. The result is the violent disintegration of
Stevie when he stumbles with the bomb in Greenwich
Park, and the immediate bringing home of the responsibility to Verloc by reason of the label, discovered among
the rags and fragments by the police, that Winnie has
sewn under the collar of Stevie's overcoat in case he should
get lost.

There follows one of the most astonishing triumphs
of genius in fiction, the final scene between Verloc and
his wife. To put it in this way, however, is misleading,
since the effect of the scene depends upon what comes
before – depends upon the cunning organization of the
whole book. We have been put in a position in which we
can't fail to realize that, by the sudden knowledge of the
death into which Verloc had led Stevie ('might be father
and son', she had fondly remarked, seeing them go off
together), Winnie's 'moral nature had been subjected to
a shock of which, in the physical order, the most violent

earthquake of history could only be a faint and languid rendering'. And we appreciate to the full the moral insulation that has kept the Verlocs, in their decent marital domesticity, strangers to each other : 'Do be reasonable, Winnie. What would it have been if you had lost me !' Here we have the assumption on which Verloc, with magnanimous restraint (for did she not, without telling him, sew in that label which has done the mischief ?), undertakes to help his wife to achieve a more reasonable attitude towards the misadventure.

In his affairs of the heart Mr Verloc had always been carelessly generous, yet always with no other idea than that of being loved for himself. Upon this matter, his ethical notions being in agreement with his vanity, he was completely incorrigible. That this should be so in the case of his virtuous and legal connection he was perfectly certain. He had grown older, fatter, heavier, in the belief that he lacked no fascination for being loved for his own sake.

It is extraordinary ironic comedy; the tension is deadly and is to end in murder, but the ways in which Verloc's moral feeling exhibits the naïveties of its relation with his egotism are irresistibly comic. He has intense righteous indignation to work off :

'It wasn't the old Baron who would have had the wicked folly of getting me to call on him at eleven in the morning. There are two or three in this town that, if they had seen me going in, would have made no bones about knocking me on the head sooner or later. It was a silly, murderous trick to expose for nothing a man – like me.'

The development is rich, surprising and inevitable, and disturbing in its reality :

For the first time in his life he was taking that incurious woman into his confidence. The singularity of the event, the force and importance of the personal feelings aroused in the course of this confession, drove Stevie's fate clean out of Mr Verloc's mind. The boy's stuttering existence of fears and indignations, together with the violence of his end, had passed out of Mr Verloc's mental sight for a time. For that reason, when he looked up he was startled by the inappropriate character of his wife's stare. It was not a wild stare, and it was not inattentive, but its attention was peculiar and not satisfactory, inasmuch that it seemed concentrated upon some point beyond Mr Verloc's person. The impression was so strong that Mr Verloc glanced over his shoulder, There was nothing behind him : there was just the whitewashed wall. The excellent husband of Winnie Verloc saw no writing on the wall. He turned to his wife again. . . .

It is 'the note of wooing' (' "Come here," he said in a peculiar tone from his relaxed posture on the sofa') that finally gives the signal for the plunge of the knife between his ribs. That knife and its use, by the way, provide an illustration of the economy of form and pattern that gives every detail its significance. Not only does Verloc make (from his wife's point of view – 'This man took the boy away to murder him' is the refrain running through her head) offensively insensitive use of it when, during the scene, he carves and grossly devours lumps of cold meat; he actually refers to the possibility of a 'stab in the back' and so prompts her obsessed mind to the action. And early in the book Winnie, whose likeness to Stevie is significantly touched on from time to time, has had to 'take the carving knife away from the boy', who 'can't stand the notion of any cruelty' and has been excited by the atrocity literature kept for sale.

Upon the stabbing follows a gruesomely farcical coda in which the gallows-haunted Winnie, whose turn it now is to suppose herself loved for her own sake, clings round the neck of the gallant Comrade Ossipon, who is quite prepared to succeed to Comrade Verloc's bank-account, but is terrified when he discovers to what possibilities of suspicion he has laid himself open.

The scene between Verloc and his wife is balanced (to simplify with an inevitable crudeness, for the pattern is richly packed as well as subtle, and there can be no pretence of suggesting it fairly in summary) by the earlier scene between Chief Inspector Heat of the Special Crimes Department and the Assistant Commissioner. Heat is a magnificently done type, the higher-grade policeman, representative *par excellence* of Law and Order. 'Why not leave it to Heat?' asks Sir Ethelred, the great Personage, of the Assistant Commissioner.

'Because he is an old departmental hand. They have their own morality. My line of inquiry would appear to him an awful perversion of duty. For him the plain duty is to fix the guilt upon as many prominent anarchists as he can on some slight indications he had picked up in the course of his investigations on the spot; whereas I, he would say, am bent upon vindicating their innocence.'

Actually the Chief Inspector's morality is more interesting than that. When the discovery of the label on the singed rag brings the Greenwich bomb-affair home to Verloc, Heat is faced with a problem : luck having years before put Verloc in his way, he has been using this valuable source of information privately, and with great profit in respect of reputation and promotion. To follow up the clue would bring out all kinds of things and certainly destroy the source.

The incomplete explicitness of the motives in play — an incompleteness that may be said to take the positive

form of a kind of resonance of righteous feeling – is rendered with fine ironic subtlety :

He no longer considered it eminently desirable all round to
establish publicly the identity of the man who had blown
himself up that morning with such horrible completeness.
But he was not certain of the view his department would
take. A department is to those it employs a complex personality with ideas and fads of its own. It depends on the
loyal devotion of its servants, and the devoted loyalty of
trusted servants is associated with a certain amount of affec-
tionate contempt, which keeps it sweet, as it were. By a
benevolent provision of Nature no man is a hero to his
valet, or else the heroes would have to brush their own
clothes. Likewise no department appears perfectly wise to
the intimacy of its workers. A department does not know so
much as some of its servants. Being a dispassionate organism, it can never be perfectly informed. It would not be
good for its efficiency to know too much. Chief Inspector
Heat got out of the train in a state of thoughtfulness entirely untainted with disloyalty, but not quite free of that
jealous mistrust which so often springs on the ground of
perfect devotion, whether to women or to institutions.

During his interview with his chief, the Assistant Commissioner, to whom he listens 'with outward deference
(which means nothing, being a matter of duty) and in-
wardly with benevolent toleration', he settles down to the
resolution of bringing the trail of suspicion home to
Michaelis, a ticket-of-leave ex-convict who happens to be
the only thoroughly sympathetic member of the revolutionary group : ' "There will be no difficulty in getting up
sufficient evidence against *him*," he said with virtuous
complacency. "You may trust me for that, sir." ' He
can take this line with the complete assurance of his moral
judgment.

It was perfectly legal to arrest that man on the barest suspicion. It was legal and expedient on the face of it. His two
former chiefs would have seen the point at once; whereas
this one, without saying either yes or no, sat there, as if
lost in a dream. Moreover, besides being legal and expedient, the arrest of Michaelis solved a little personal difficulty
which worried Chief Inspector Heat somewhat. This difficulty had its bearing upon his reputation, upon his comfort,
and even upon the efficient performance of his duties. For
if Michaelis no doubt knew something about this outrage,
the Chief Inspector was fairly certain that he did not know
too much. This was just as well. He knew much less – the
Chief Inspector was positive – than certain other individuals he had in his mind, but whose arrest seemed to him
inexpedient, besides being a more complicated matter, on
account of the rules of the game. The rules of the game did
not protect so much Michaelis who was an ex-convict. It
would be stupid not to take advantage of legal facilities. . . .

When the Assistant Commissioner disconcerts him with
an undepartmental scepticism ('Now what is it you've
got up your sleeve?'), Heat is not only very annoyed
("You, my boy," he said to himself . . . "you, my boy,
you don't know your place, and your place won't know
you very long either, I bet" '), he is morally outraged :

He had discovered in this affair a delicate and perplexing
side, forcing upon the discoverer a certain amount of in-
sincerity which, under the names of skill, prudence, dis-
cretion, turns up at one point or another in most human
affairs. He felt at the moment like a tight-rope artist might
feel if suddenly, in the middle of the performance, the mana-
ger of the Music Hall were to rush out of the proper mana-
gerial seclusion and begin to shake the rope.

His indignation responds musically, as it were, to that of
Comrade Ossipon (along with a great deal else) when

he hears of the bomb-explosion, and exclaims that 'under the present circumstances it's nothing short of criminal'.

Heat has a further reason for not following up the clue. He has just, in one of the most memorable of the many vivid and pregnant scenes and episodes in the book, had his chance meeting in the narrow by-street with the Professor, who made the bomb. The Chief Inspector is not in any case in his element where revolutionists are concerned:

At the beginning of his career Chief Inspector Heat had been concerned with the more energetic forms of thieving. He had gained his spurs in that sphere, and naturally enough had kept for it, after his promotion to another department, a feeling not very far removed from affection. Thieving was not a sheer absurdity. It was a form of human industry, perverse indeed, but still an industry exercised in an industrious world; it was work undertaken for the same reason as the work in potteries, in coal mines, in fields, in tool-grinding shops. It was labour, whose practical difference from the other forms of labour consisted in the nature of its risk, which did not lie in ankylosis, or lead-poisoning, or fire-damp, or gritty dust, but in what may be briefly defined in its own special phraseology as 'Seven years hard'. Chief Inspector Heat was, of course, not insensible to the gravity of moral differences. But neither were the thieves he had been looking after. They submitted to the severe sanctions of a morality familiar to Chief Inspector Heat with a certain resignation. They were his fellow-citizens gone wrong because of imperfect education Chief Inspector Heat believed; but allowing for that difference, he could understand the mind of a burglar, because, as a matter of fact, the mind and the instincts of a burglar are of the same kind as the mind and the instincts of a police officer. Both recognize the same conventions and have a working knowledge of each other's methods and of the routine of their respective trades. They understand each other, which is advantageous to both, and establishes a sort of amenity in their relations. Products of the same machine, one classed as useful and the other as noxious, they take the machine for granted in different ways, but with a seriousness essentially the same.

The Professor, physically insignificant, but happy in the superiority given him by the bomb he always carries on his person and by his reputation for a reckless readiness to touch it off rather than be arrested, represents revolutionary abnormality in its most disconcerting and repugnant form :

After paying this tribute to what is normal in the constitution of society (for the idea of thieving appeared to his instinct as normal as the idea of property), Chief Inspector Heat felt very angry with himself for having stopped. . . .

The encounter did not leave behind with Inspector Heat that satisfactory sense of superiority the members of the police force get from the unofficial but intimate side of their intercourse with the criminal classes, by which the vanity of power is soothed, and the vulgar love of domination over our fellow-creatures is flattered as worthily as it deserves.

The perfect anarchist was not recognized as a fellow-creature by Chief Inspector Heat. He was impossible – a mad dog to be left alone. . . . This being the strong feeling of Inspector Heat, it appeared to him just and proper that this affair should be shunted off its obscure and inconvenient track, leading goodness knows where, into a quiet (and lawful) siding called Michaelis.

Conrad himself shows an unmistakable dislike of revolutionists. In *The Secret Agent* he explains them mainly in terms of indolence (though the Professor and Michaelis are contrasting and complementary special cases). In *Under Western Eyes* (1911), which comes up for notice next, his revolutionists are Russians, and, while his pre-

entment is hardly more flattering, his general reflections
.re on different lines:

. . in a real revolution – not a simple dynastic change or a
nere reform of institutions – in a real revolution the best
haracters do not come to the front. A violent revolution
alls into the hands of narrow-minded fanatics and of tyran-
.ical hypocrites at first. Afterwards comes the turn of all
he pretentious intellectual failures of the time. Such are
he chiefs and the leaders. You will notice that I have left
.ut the mere rogues. The scrupulous and the just, the noble,
.umane, and devoted natures; the unselfish and the in-
elligent may begin a movement – but it passes away from
hem. They are not the leaders of a revolution. They are its
.ictims : the victims of disgust, of disenchantment – often
.f remorse. Hopes grotesquely betrayed, ideals caricatured
– that is the definition of revolutionary successes. There
.ave been in every revolution hearts broken by such suc-
.esses.'

The old teacher of languages, the presence in the story
.f 'Western eyes', is here warning Natalia, sister of Haldin
he heroic assassin; and the revolutionists we are shown –
Bearers [comments Razumov] of the spark to start an
xplosion which is meant to change fundamentally the
.ives of so many millions in order that Peter Ivanovitch
hould be the head of a state' – leave no room for doubt
hat he speaks for Conrad. In Peter Ivanovitch, 'the
.eroic fugitive', eloquent, woman-exploiting egoist, and
Russian Mazzini', we have, we suspect, an actual his-
.orical person.

The space given to *The Secret Agent* doesn't leave
nuch for *Under Western Eyes*. *The Secret Agent* is one
.f Conrad's two supreme masterpieces, one of the two
.nquestionable classics of the first order that he added to
he English novel, and, in its own way, it is like *Nostromo*

T.S.A.—E

in the subtle and triumphant complexity of its art -
like, too, in not having had due critical recognition. *Under*
Western Eyes cannot be claimed with the same confidence
for that order, though it is a most distinguished work, and
must be counted among those upon which Conrad's status
as one of the great English masters securely rests. It is
related to *The Secret Agent* not only by the revolutionists, but by the theme of isolation (for this figures a great
deal in that book – Winnie Verloc jumps to her death
from the night Channel-steamer at least as much to escape
the void in which Stevie's death followed by Ossipon's
desertion has left her as from fear of the gallows). *Under*
Western Eyes has for theme moral isolation as represented
by the case of the Russian student Razumov. . . .

Source : *The Great Tradition: George Eliot, Henry*
            James, Joseph Conrad (1948), pp. 209–21.

V. S. Pritchett

AN ÉMIGRÉ (1953)

The daily evil of the émigré is his isolation. He has lost the main ground of the moral life: that we do not live until we live in others. The temptations that face him are embittering to any man capable of reflection: he can live in the past; he can become an uprooted dilettante; he can cultivate, in the words of Heyst in Joseph Conrad's *Victory*, that 'form of contempt called pity' which comes easily to the isolated man; he can regard anarchy as the ruling spirit in the world. Crime may come nearer to his fingers and, with less obstruction, to his imagination than it does to rooted people. In a world like our own, the solicitations of the police, the secret agent, the revolutionary, the traitor, are very likely, under one guise or another, to come his way. No doubt these extreme enticements are evaded by most émigrés, who alleviate the sense of persecution by living in the past and keep their nostalgias and their rancours indoors; but, mild or extreme, they unite to force upon the isolated man his main addiction. He becomes pre-eminently a conscience.

Isolation and conscience are the dominant motifs in the novels of Joseph Conrad and, two of them especially, *The Secret Agent* and *Under Western Eyes*, become more and more suggestive to the contemporary reader. They attract because they are free from that sudden fogginess, that enlarged bad temper which Conrad called Destiny, and from the melodrama or rhetoric, which play tricks with the lighting and climate of many of his ambitious works. They have the compactness, the efficiency of that peculiarly modern form of writing, the thriller with a bitter moral flavour. And they put a central modern question to ourselves – what is our attitude to treachery and other moral consequences of a belief in revolution?

Conrad's terms are out of date, of course, though not as seriously as might be thought. Anarchists do not throw bombs in London; in Russia, the tyrant is not assassinated. But the essentials of European history have not changed since the Eighties of last century; what was talked about has simply come true. The revolutionary thug who has the fine art of bursting Razumov's ear drums in *Under Western Eyes* is an anthropoid forerunner of thousands who have gone one better than that in the police states. Conrad is a reactionary; for him the old despotism and the new Utopianism are complementary forms of moral anarchy. Their end is cynicism, more despotism, more destruction, and to that opinion some have now reluctantly come. But Conrad was a fixed reactionary; he had never tried to tack across the revolutionary tide; he hated the Russian revolution as a Pole who was already a generation away from the hatred of his time; his hatred was glued into the past. The positive contribution of his political views is that they double the precision of our dilemmas of conscience by presenting them in reverse. The weakness – let us get it over at once. Conrad's judgment is true and untrue, but what he said of Heyst in *Victory* points out the weakness:

The young man learned to reflect, which is a destructive process, a reckoning of the cost. It is not the clear-sighted who lead the world. Great achievements are accomplished in a blessed warm mental fog.

Conrad is an exile. He is not committed except to pessi

mism. He is, for private and public reasons, tortured by the danger of becoming a moral dilettante. Because he is so excruciatingly aware of all the half shades of that case, he has his authority.

Razumov in *Under Western Eyes* is a sympathetic character. He is the recurring 'lonely' being in Conrad's novels. Another Conradian theme, perhaps Slavonic and certainly Romantic : he has a 'double' in Haldin, the student assassin. 'In times of mental and political unrest', the Razumovs of the world keep

an instinctive hold on normal, practical everyday life. He was aware of the emotional tension of his time; he even responded to it in an indefinite way. But his main concern was with his work, his studies and with his own future.

Not a prig, not a careerist, not dull; he is intelligent and sensitive. His worse fault is a bad temper which comes from one of Stendhal's definitions of misfortune : 'Not having the evils of his age' – if we can use the word 'age' in a double sense. The irrational driving force in him comes from insecurity and loneliness; he is a bastard. Just when Razumov's good resolutions are ripe, Haldin the terrorist hides in his room and, by the very contact, dooms Razumov to eternal political suspicion. There follows a scene in which Conrad's highest dramatic gifts as a novelist are brought, uncorrupted, into play : the picture of the student's room, Razumov's despairing journey through the snow at night to the inn to fetch the cab driver who will enable the exalted assassin to escape, Razumov's discovery that the man is dead drunk; and then the journey back in which, having failed, Razumov revolts against his unjust situation and his own quietism, changes his mind and betrays Haldin to the police. The scene is a very long one and also exposes Conrad's weakness – the creaking sentence, the rumble of stage scenery and some staginess of dialogue.

Conrad wrote *Under Western Eyes* perhaps to bring a harder Western focus upon a theme of Dostoevsky. There is an evident Polish contempt for the lack of fixed positions in the Russian mind; or, at any rate, an ironical wonder at its readiness for cynicism. With brilliant ingenuity he caps scene after scene with its opposite. The exalted assassin is plainly sensitive about the 'greatness' of his action. Razumov has acted from a sense of right and discovers even *that* will not be its own reward; exile alone is possible. Guilt (as always in Conrad) marks the drifter. Yet even exile is poisoned, though not by remorse; it is poisoned because the authorities can now force Razumov to become a spy on the revolutionaries as the price of concealing his act. Razumov is obliged to take on the mind of a guilty man when, by his morality, he is virtuous; in doing so, and by contact with Haldin's young sister in Geneva, he comes to see the innocent and honourable illusions that precede conversion to revolutionary action. The inevitable Russian confession follows, not because Razumov has changed his mind, but because he longs for moral freedom.

What is contemporary in this book is the response to seediness, treachery, slackness and corruption. This response is the direct product of the last words of Heyst in *Victory*: 'Woe to the man whose heart has not learned while young to hope, to love – and to put his trust in life.' Conrad himself found a strong if not lasting interest in the order and discipline of life at sea, and his scorn is softened in *Under Western Eyes* by the attempt of one kind of Slav to understand another. In *The Secret Agent* there is no such emotional entanglement; his scorn, unrestrained, now becomes almost overpoweringly rich and pungent and his irony leaves nothing standing.

The masters of Conrad's day were Meredith and Stevenson, and Conrad's book about the lazy agent-provocateur who gets his feeble-minded brother-in-law killed by mistake shows the strong influence of these writers. *The Secret Agent* is a thriller, a very artificial form of writing which realism rarely redeems from its fundamental fantasy. No thriller can be believed, and even when meaning and psychological ingredients are put into it, its people and events cannot really bear the weight. *The Secret Agent* begins with the incredible character of Vladimir, the absurd, highly-stylised intellectual plotter, and the artifice is at odds with the truly real and powerful elements in the book: the descriptions of London, the portraits of those perfect if intellectually diagnosed Londoners, Mrs Verloc, her mother and Stevie. Outside of this warm, human centre Conrad is dangerously exhibitionist. Here conscience has its sardonic comedies and he seems superbly to be showing off his obsession with the dirtiness, the shabbiness of foolish or dishonoured minds: 'His descent into the street was like the descent into a slimy aquarium from which the water has been run off.' A detail like that – and Conrad is a master of image – describes a London street and defines the book. Verloc's birth-control shop takes one down and down to the grubbiness of London's back streets and the pathetic vulgarities of cheap civilisation.

Conrad's genius was for picturesque discussion rather than for narrative – he was tortured, one is told, by the difficulties of invention – and what always impresses is his rummaging about, back and forth, in the lives of his characters. Verloc, the agent, is wonderful in his laziness, his dull humour, his amorousness, his commonplaceness and his injured vanity. It was a master stroke to make this destroyer respectable and to pounce upon the isolation – once more, the Conrad theme – in which this foolish member of the French-letter trade lived. Towards the end, when the idiot Stevie has been killed through Verloc's irresponsibility, it is wonderful that Verloc quite unblinkingly expects the tragedy to make no difference to his relations with his wife. After all, she has got *him*! The murder is not well done. It is, in fact, too cleverly done, with an eye for all the effects, and shows Conrad at his most self-conscious. The crime is in keeping with the contrived tone of the book, the general unsavoury sapience; but the author's irony is too much with us. Mrs Verloc is as wonderful as the husband she kills. She is a simple, reserved woman, governed by the desire for security, living on two or three strong and usually concealed feelings. Her words, in the London way, rarely reveal what these are; in fact the way in which she talks off the beat of her feelings the whole time is well-observed. But when she discovers that her husband is a monster, that he is a worse monster because he does not realise it or does not see why *that* should upset his domestic bliss; when she realises he is a moral idiot and that his reply to grief is 'Let her have her cry. I'll go to bed with her, that'll put her right', a terrifying woman rises up with a carving knife in her hand. Afterwards, it is perfect that she relapses into the simple resource of a feminine guile, so pathetically vain, that a crude crook can do her down as easy as winking.

Heat, the police superintendent, is another sound portrait. His Assistant Commissioner belongs to the dubious higher moral reaches which thriller writers have a perennial fancy for: contact with crime and the police sows in them the desire to have everything taped: God comes to Scotland Yard. The Assistant Commissioner, one notices, has the now professional 'sense of loneliness, of evil freedom', but this is, at the last moment, made real to us by one of those sardonic afterthoughts by which Conrad

saves himself from sentimentality. The Assistant Commissioner, we are told, finds 'the sense of loneliness and evil
freedom *rather pleasant*'. This is indeed why he is an
Assistant Commissioner : he is a hunter. (It is always, in
Conrad, the small additional comment that puts on the
rounding and convincing touch.)

Conrad, the exile, the isolated man, was the master of
any atmosphere. That gift comes at once to the sensibility
of the émigré. Like the French novelists, like Meredith
and Henry James, he moves in narrative from idea to
idea, to the change in moral climate rather than from
event to event. The first part of *Under Western Eyes*
comes beautifully to a close on Councillor Milukin's short
inquiry when Razumov says he is going to retire :
'Where to?' Obviously there is nowhere. Conrad's novels
are marked by such crucial sentences, which change a
whole view of life, and his dramas are the dramas of the
change of view. Conrad, the dilettante, takes the soul or
the conscience, and tries them now in this position, now
that; a new Good means a new guilt. Heyst in *Victory*
knows the reason : the son of a brilliant man who has
seen through all human values, Heyst is a born exile in a
world that shocks. His aim must be to avoid committal.
But like the Captain in *The Secret Sharer* who has the
runaway hidden in his cabin, Conrad also has the committed 'double' in his life. This dichotomy provides the
drama and the rich substance of his books.

SOURCE : *Books in General* (1953) pp. 216–22.

Irving Howe

CONRAD:
ORDER AND ANARCHY (1957)

In *Under Western Eyes* the recommendation to charity is heeded on occasion, in *The Secret Agent* hardly at all. The secret agent is Mr Verloc, employed by the Czarist embassy to spy upon a group of harmless, aimless and witless London anarchists. To gain a life of comfort Mr Verloc has chosen the profession of informer and despite the revolutionary phrases he must mouth, comfort is all he wants. He is entirely respectable in his social impulses, he would no more think of violating the prevalent norms than of submitting to heavy labor, and his scorn for the anarchist chatterboxes with whom he must associate is proper enough to satisfy the most exacting philistine. But Mr Verloc's ease comes to an abrupt stop when his employer prods him to commit an outrage meant to force the British government into abandoning its tolerance of refugee radicals. Cursing the fate – he cannot distinguish between indolence and destiny – that has led him to gamble his life on borrowed rhetoric, Mr Verloc stumbles into a nightmare of calamities and then, a squalid death. As with so many other characters in Conrad, his destruction follows from his desire – the desire of a moderate man – to insulate himself from the complications of the great world.

The very conception of Mr Verloc is brilliantly original, a fine example of Conrad's gift for noticing the threads of the ridiculous as they weave their way through political life. (A gift that is likely to be cultivated by people who look with discomfort upon their political past.) 'There isn't a murdering plot for the last eleven years,' wails Mr Verloc in the voice of a clerk suddenly cashiered, 'that I haven't had my finger in at the risk of my life. There's scores of these revolutionists I've sent off with bombs in their blamed pockets to get themselves caught on the frontier.' For even as he acts the informer, that most lonely of vocations and until recently the least honored, Mr Verloc remains a dull-minded complying Englishman, a beef-and-ale patriot whose ordinariness has served, by a wild curve of irony, to place him beyond the limits of ordinary society.

Nothing in the novel is equal to this opening invention, but there are moments which show Conrad's corrosive genius at something very close to its best. *The Secret Agent* is a work of enormous possibilities, far from fully realized but realized just enough to enable us to see how Conrad thwarts and denies his own gifts. At times his ability to make the life of humanity seem a thing of shame reaches an appalling completeness – as, most strikingly, in the conversation between Mr Verloc and his wife the moment before she plunges a knife into his ribs. Reading such passages – it is they that prompt me to speak of Conrad's genius as 'corrosive' – one feels overwhelmed before the power that sheer fatuousness can exert upon man's destiny. But Conrad pushes too hard. The final meeting between Mr Verloc and his wife, dazzling *tour de force* though it may be, shatters the structure of the novel; Conrad's insistence upon squeezing the last ounce of sordid absurdity from their relationship is in conflict with the narrative rhythm of the book. He lacks the talent for self-resistance that is indispensable to a novelist for whom irony has been transformed from a tactic into a total perspective.

Few things in the novel, or in all of Conrad, are more
gloomily impressive than the care with which he demon-
strates that every part of society is implicated in Mr Verloc's fate and responsible for Stevie's death. Since *The
Secret Agent* is a novel in which the sense of nausea is at
least as powerful as the claims of indignation or even
pity, there is no unavoidable obligation to regard it as
an indictment of anything; but if there is an indictment,
it is total. The anarchists and the Russians – their guilt
is obvious enough, and in Conrad perilously close to the
banal; but the English too are implicated, their moderation, before which Conrad so frequently abandons all
critical judgment, now being seen as a form of obtuse-
ness as well as a quality of civilization.

Thomas Mann, who regards *The Secret Agent* as an
expression of Conrad's uneasy Anglophilism, finds in the
novel 'the whole conflict between the British and the Russian political ideology'. He is right, but only up to a point.
Frightened and appalled by everything he regards as dis-
tinctively 'European', Conrad repeatedly hurries back to
the comforts of English moderation; but in the end even
the English do not come off very well, for if they are not
guilty of the crimes committed by the Russians and the
anarchists, they are guilty of a stupidity and complacence
which renders them accessories to these crimes. Inspector
Heat, having made a good thing out of Mr Verloc, hates
to see his man endangered: one must think of one's
career, and for the careers of policemen secret agents are
indispensable. The Inspector's outlook, which is simply
that of the official mind, is magnified and parodied in
the great elder statesman Sir Ethelred. When this living
monument to the genius of England is told by the Assistant Commissioner that

'This is an imperfect world –'

The deep-voiced presence on the hearthrug, motionless, with big elbows stuck out, said hastily :

'Be lucid, please.'

Against the English Conrad's half-affectionate complaint is that they are too stolid, too untrained in the imagination of disaster, to understand the dangers that are threatening the civilized world. It is a familiar complaint.

The Secret Agent is the work of a man who looks upon the political spectacle – as, a little too often, the whole of life – from a great and chilling distance, and who needs to keep that distance in order to survive. Conrad's growing alienation from the modes and assumptions of modern society, which has nothing in common with literary fashion but is an utterly serious response, seems to me profoundly impressive; too often, however, the impressiveness has more to do with sociological and ethical statement than literary value. Conrad's critical distance, the sense he communicates of writing as a man who has *cut himself off*, may win our sympathy, but it has unhappy consequences for the novel. He tends to become stiff, even rigid, in his rejections, and the novel resembles, at times, a relentless mill in which character after character is being ground to dust. The sense of a *They* – whatever in the outer world imperils and destroys human life – is overwhelming; the sense of a *We* – whatever in ourselves can resist this enemy – is extremely faint. And I say this not primarily on moral grounds, though that would not seem to me at all irrelevant, but out of a consideration of the local needs of the novel. What one misses in *The Secret Agent* is some dramatic principle of contradiction, some force of resistance; in a word, a moral positive to serve literary ends. Conrad's ironic tone suffuses every sentence, nagging at our attention to the point where one yearns for the relief of direct statement almost as if it were an ethical good.

And this is true even for Conrad's development of the theme that the most deviant political figures are driven to destruction by their desire, shared with the vast sluggish mass of men, for normal and domestic convenience. That the very motives which lead one man to a suburb can entangle another in a conspiracy, that the extremists of politics can be as mediocre in their personal standards as those who find safety in the cant of political moderation – this is a brilliant insight. And yet in its very brilliance, it disfigures the novel. *The Secret Agent* is surrounded by a thick fog of irony which steadily eats away at the features, the energies, the very vitals of its major characters. What the English narrator does in *Under Western Eyes,* Conrad's style overdoes in *The Secret Agent.* It is one thing for a novelist gradually to deprive his characters of their pretensions or illusions, another thing to deny them the mildest claims to dignity and redemption. The novel forces one to conclude either that Conrad's fable is not worth troubling about, which I take to be manifestly untrue, or that his irony has turned in upon itself, becoming facile through its pervasiveness and lack of grading. The qualifications required by irony are present in abundance, but it is difficult to determine *what* is being qualified, which standard of behavior is being singled out for attack or defense. So peevish an irony must have its source less in zeal or anger than in some deep distemper.

Only one character escapes this heavy irony, and that is Stevie the idiot boy, a literary cousin of Dostoevsky's Myshkin. But unlike Myshkin, poor Stevie cannot support the weight of suffering thrust upon him, for where Dostoevsky's idiot grazes the sublime Conrad's never emerges from the pitiable. Stevie's history is acutely worked in, but he figures merely as a prepared victim, the irony which drenches all the others never so much as touching him. He is meant to convey a purity of pathos and to represent the humanitarian impulse in its most vulnerable form; but a character for whom one feels nothing but pity can hardly command the emotion Conrad intends.

Where Conrad presumes to render the London anarchists in their characteristic haunts and accents, he drops to a coarse-spirited burlesque. That the anarchists whom the Czarist embassy fears should prove to be inept and impotent is part of Conrad's ironic intent, and for purposes of the novel an entirely acceptable intent; but the burlesque is too vindictive, the malice too cruel. Seldom did Conrad miscalculate so badly as in his view of the bomb-laden 'Professor'. To Cunninghame Graham he wrote that the Professor was not meant to be 'despicable . . . I wanted to give him a note of perfect sincerity'; yet it is difficult to regard this grimy lunatic as anything but a cartoon. The defect, as Conrad was later to say about another revolutionary in *The Rover*, 'is, alas, in the treatment, which instead of half-pathetic makes him half-grotesque'.

Anarchists, wrote Conrad, are motivated by a 'dislike of all kinds of recognized labour'. One need hardly be a partisan of the anarchist movement to grant that with regard to such of its leaders as Kropotkin and Bakunin this estimate is a fabulous vulgarity. Not only does Conrad fail to account for the fascination they obviously hold for him, he removes any reasonable ground for the fear they also arouse in him. For if it be irony to portray them as garrulous fools, a stricter irony would allow fools a hidden strength.[1]

From Conrad's letters one gathers that some of his friends questioned him about his treatment of radical

characters. To Cunninghame Graham he replied: 'I
don't think I've been satirizing the revolutionary world.
All these people are not revolutionists – they are mere
shams.' And to John Galsworthy: 'The whole thing is
superficial and but a tale. I had no idea to consider Anarchism politically or to treat it in its philosophical aspect;
as a manifestation of human nature in its discontent and
imbecility.'

These disclaimers do not satisfy. To plead that the
anarchists of *The Secret Agent* are mere shams and therefore no reflection on the radical world, is to evade the
question: why does Conrad habitually populate that
world with shams? and even more important, doesn't his
association of anarchist and sham deprive him of access
to the complexities of the radical mind? Conrad's
'esthetic' defense, that he was merely writing a piece of
fiction, would have been scorned by Dostoevsky, as by
most great writers; Dostoevsky would surely have insisted
that his novels, far from being mere tales, were expres-
sions of fundamental truth.

These remarks bring us, unavoidably, to the slippery
problem of the relation between a novel and actuality.
In our fiercely partisan age it is difficult to read books
like *Under Western Eyes* or *The Secret Agent* without
fiercely partisan emotions. No matter what their authors
intend, such novels serve rhetorical ends, persuading toward one or another point of view. In practice it is hard
to make the Aristotelian distinction between the imaginative and the rhetorical, since an author's vision, or imaginative quality, depends partly on his beliefs, or
rhetorical ends. And the critic too had better acknowledge that he comes to the political novel with an eye that
is partial and perhaps inflamed.

That a novel includes an accurate report of an historical
event is not necessarily a point in its favor. What would

be a point in its favor is the presence of that quality we loosely call 'true to life', or here more pertinently, true to the moral complexities of political behavior. This quality may be had by modelling a novel on actual events, but if that is so it merely explains how good novels are sometimes written, not why they are good. A casual explanation should not be taken as a ground for valuation.

But if a close adherence to actual events is sometimes necessary for writing a good novel, the mere accurate transcription of those events is not a sufficient condition for declaring it good (thus we say, 'he has the facts right but misses the spirit completely'). Still, when a critic praises a novel for giving an accurate picture of the nineteenth-century anarchist movement he may be making, through ellipsis or clumsiness, a valid point in its behalf, namely, that it does communicate a sense of the moral complexities of political behavior.

A person without any knowledge of the anarchists might come to see that Conrad's treatment of them is warped or at least dubious. But even here his experience would shape his judgment, he would be testing the life of the novel by his sense of life. As critics we may claim to be interested only in the life that is *in* the novel, but we cannot engage in this formal apprehension except as we bring to our reading some mature sense of what is living and what is dead. And this holds true, though in a more complicated way, for fantasy, surrealism and other non-realistic modes.

Since the novel is concerned with what 'really happens', with the essential or the probable, it must have some correspondence to what *has* happened. So to say that a novel which contains characters called 'anarchists' and is set in 'the nineteenth century' does not give an accurate picture of nineteenth-century anarchism, *may* be a way of making, elliptically, a judgment against the

novel. It may be a way of saying that the events in the
novel, partly because they are too different from what has
happened in such circumstances, are not sufficiently like
what 'really happens' in those circumstances.

As a novelist Conrad is under no obligation to admire
the anarchists or accept their doctrine; he need not give a
faithful report of their history, and he may even, without
excessive jeopardy, distort some of the facts about them.
But he cannot, short of damaging his book, violate our
sense of what 'really happens' in the kind of world that is
summoned by the world 'anarchist'.

With *Nostromo* we come to a work of the first rank, much
wider in social scope and more delicately balanced in
point of view than either *The Secret Agent* or *Under
Western Eyes*. *Nostromo* lacks – it does not strive for –
the virtuoso flashes of *The Secret Agent*, and except for
the haunting night scene in the Placid Gulf, it cannot
equal the intensity of the first 100 pages of *Under Western
Eyes*.[2]

SOURCE: *Politics and the Novel* (1957) pp. 93–100.

NOTES

1. In *The Great Tradition* F. R. Leavis reports that 'Q'
once told him Henry James 'didn't know the right people'.
A fair point, concedes Mr Leavis: 'after all, the admirable
types, the public spirit and serious culture . . . were characteristic products of the England of "the best families" of
James' time. Why does he seem to know nothing about this
real and most impressive best?' A chapter later Mr Leavis
notes, without a tremor of disturbance, Conrad's opinion
that the anarchists were inspired mainly by laziness. It is
interesting that a critic ready to chastise James for harsh-

ness toward the landowning class should not also wonder whether Conrad neglected 'the real and most impressive best' among the nineteenth-century anarchists.

2. [Editor's Note.] This excerpt (*Politics and the Novel*, pp. 93–100) reproduces the third section of the chapter 'Conrad : Order and Anarchy' and the first sentence of the fourth. The essay was first published in *Kenyon Review*, xv (1953) 505–12, and xvi (1954) 1–9.

Albert J. Guérard

A VERSION OF ANARCHY (1958)

The Secret Agent (1907) and *Under Western Eyes* (1911) stand appealingly between the visionary, experimental early masterpieces and the sentimentalities of *Chance* and *Victory*. This does not mean that Conrad (tired as he certainly was, ridden by sickness and debt) had already entered into an uninterrupted decline. Neither of these fine political novels shows such lapses in language as occurred in the third part of *Nostromo*; neither shows the clumsiness which comes from radical imaginative fatigue. But they are transitional books in the over-all movement from an eccentric to a popularized art and from a highly personal view of humanity to a normalized one. This is true even though the astounding complications of *Chance* are still to come. For already much of the personal rhythm, audacity of rhetoric, and strangeness of perspective have been lost. In part 'lost', no doubt; in part deliberately sacrificed to the recognition that things must be made easier for the reader; and in part repudiated. It is obvious that Conrad made a conscious effort to chasten and simplify style, to subdue temperamental evasiveness and control digressive fantasy. And some of this effort (though Conrad's mind and letters now turned rather desperately to the question of finding a larger public) must be attributed to sincere artistic conviction. *The Secret Agent* and *Under Western Eyes* are intelligent, carefully planned novels showing a major change from the impressionist to the realist method.

They also show a new mastery of suspenseful plotting, a new power to dramatize scene and crisis directly, a full command of pure nonidiosyncratic English. In a word they show, *The Secret Agent* especially, control. *The Secret Agent* is, among Conrad's full-length novels, the first easy one and perhaps the only one to know fairly well what it is doing from the first sentence to the last. But even the great first and fourth parts of *Under Western Eyes* (where darker energies are engaged) are comparatively straightforward.

Such a normalizing of method might well betoken and reflect a normalizing of attitude; or, as it is sometimes miscalled, a maturing of attitude. The artist sees matters less obsessively but also less freshly; the world falls back into the place common sense gives it. There are several indications that such a normalizing was occurring in Conrad, who in 1907 was fifty years old. The political subject was given fairly uninhibited and fantastic treatment in the stories of *A Set of Six*; the material of 'The Informer' and even of 'An Anarchist' would be used in certain pages of *The Secret Agent*. But by then the vision of moral anarchy and latent violence had come under full control and achieved expository clarity. The very turn to the political subject means a normalizing of interest, after all; so too does the turn to comedy with its implications of a rational or social norm and its objective interest in behavior. *The Secret Agent* is macabre comedy, and it would be possible to present it as the very darkest of Conrad's books: a version of modern life and modern man untouched by grace in any form except that of British legality; a vision (in his own words) 'of a monstrous town . . . a cruel devourer of the world's light'; a book about mankind's petty weakness and infirmity of spirit. And yet it is comedy: the public, the nonsolipsistic art. The entirely rational author watches with amusement and scorn the respectability of the criminal and the laziness of the violent, and watches Verloc's blind egoism bring on his own ludicrous destruction.

The interest in politics and the turn to a kind of comedy are accompanied, in *The Secret Agent*, by another sign of normalization: the close attention and sympathy given Winnie Verloc, and the very fact that she has been so successfully created. Conrad claimed she was the book's imaginative center. But the portrait is not entirely free of the old misogyny; the attention at last becomes (like that of Comrade Ossipon himself) a terrified, 'scandalized' attention. *Under Western Eyes* rather shows the real advance toward an understanding at once mature and compassionate of women; there is not a trace of gratuitous or obsessive denigration in the lifelike portraits of Nathalie Haldin, Mrs Haldin, Tekla, or even Sophia Antonovna. Some of this new assurance and security in the presence of the female menace may be due to the Jamesian position and Jamesian tone of the narrator: a man clearly too old for a serious romance with Nathalie, and whose role is to *watch* her affectionately. Misogynous reveries are less likely where at least one spokesman for the author has withdrawn from the start. As for Razumov (with whom Conrad certainly identified more closely) – his nominal interest in Nathalie, as soul to be damaged or woman to be loved, cannot be taken very seriously. The matter is above sex. She is instead another major witness in his interior drama of self-scrutiny and self-destruction.

These easier and more conventional realistic novels were, nevertheless, commercial failures. Conrad blamed some of this failure on the 'sordid surroundings' of *The Secret Agent* and on the 'detachment' of *Under Western Eyes*. But it may be that they failed for the very reason that makes them so accessible to us: that they were some twenty years ahead of their time and, *The Secret Agent* especially, virtually created the genre of the serious psycho-political mystery novel. They recognized that the melodramatic fringe of society (the world of connivance between police and petty criminal, of *agent-provocateur* and police informer, of thought-crime and torture and confession, of anarchist and revolutionary exile) could also be, symbolically and morally, at the very heart of society and corrupting it. But the genteel reader in a confident Edwardian England could hardly be expected to take such 'recognitions' seriously, or to accept Conrad's very dim view of humanitarian gesture, or to see a real connection between international affairs and introspective torments. *The Secret Agent* dealt, after all, with a few Soho crackpots and *Under Western Eyes* with a few Russian crackpots in Geneva! The actual events (an attempt to blow up the Greenwich Observatory, the assassination of Plehve) were safely in the past. It has taken the fiction of Greene, Moravia, Flaiano, Koestler, and others, not to mention the Second World War and its aftermath, to connect fully private conscience and public political crime; to convince us that the moral anarchies and cynicisms and betrayals on which Conrad insisted are realities not ornaments of a fiction. And are never safely in the past.

Various readers have remarked on *The Secret Agent*'s anticipation of Graham Greene, and on the Dostoevskian character of *Under Western Eyes*. But Greene is not Dostoevsky. It is well to make this distinction at the outset, and to recognize that *Under Western Eyes* is the greater novel of the two. Mr Leavis' preference for *The Secret Agent* (which leaves it not far short of that summit of the English novel *Hard Times*) is to be explained, I suppose, by a preference for neatness of construction and for explicit development of a morally serious theme. But *Under Western Eyes* is more than this, more than a work of fine satirical intelligence. It is, except for the brief *Shadow Line*, the last book in which Conrad was importantly involved and also the last in which he could, importantly not sentimentally, involve his readers. It contains those unpredictables and audacities which may indicate very strong engagement and which, if they turn out to be true and persuasive, provide one of the surest ways of distinguishing the work of powerful imagination from the intelligent imitation of life. And *Under Western Eyes* is tragedy. It is tragedy dealing beyond its private issue with the most contemporary of the ancient conflicts, the essential one: that between the individual ethic of personal loyalty and the public 'ethic of state'. The particular occasion of a man fallen under the shadow of Russian autocracy is also contemporary enough. The novel's enormous personal achievement is to have done so much justice to Russia and things Russian. It reminds us, as we recall Conrad's hatreds and disgusts, how great must have been the share of conscious imaginative integrity as well as how great the devil's share of unconscious sympathy.

The Secret Agent (subtitled 'A Simple Tale') is a work to be enjoyed, and to be enjoyed thoughtfully. But it is not an intimate personal experience to be shared and survived, nor a political treatise to be endlessly reread and debated. 'After all, you must not take it too seriously. The whole thing is superficial and it is but a tale. I had no idea to consider Anarchism politically, or to treat it seriously in its philosophical aspect. . . . The general reflections whether right or wrong are not meant as bolts. . . . They are, if anything, mere digs at the people in the tale.' Such disclaimers as these can be irritating, as when a difficult symbolist claims he wants only to 'tell a story'. But Conrad seems to be speaking with some sincerity in this letter to Galsworthy; or when, to his publisher, he describes the novel as purely a work of imagination without social or philosophical intention. This is doubtless too strong a statement. But the word *entertainment* comes to mind in the honorable sense given it by Graham Greene : an exciting story for thoughtful readers, and in which the most serious and most intimate human concerns (such as alcoholism and bodily degradation, political loyalty and international conflict, even religious conversion and neurotic self-destructiveness) are put to dramatic and 'entertaining' use. This does not mean that Greene does not intend quite sincerely his wry general reflections and religious asides, but simply that they subserve the major aim of original and successful entertainment. (I would not even except the sincere *Quiet American*, a fine dramatized essay, though I would except large portions of the great *Power and the Glory*.) Briefly, one of the appeals of Greene's fiction derives from the expository play of an interesting and sardonic mind. But the books were not written for the sake of this expository play. Nor were they written to convert readers.

The situation in *The Secret Agent* is similar. The novel does have its genuine seriousness of theme; it does express certain strong and austere convictions, recognizably the author's. But it neither explores these convictions for subtle ramification and nuance, nor ever seriously challenges them. Instead, the convictions are simple and forcefully affirmed. Thus the notable absence of strong emotional involvement with any one character is accompanied by a relative absence of subtle intellectual conflict. The Gides and the Thomas Manns, lovers of intellectual play for its own sake, are capable of questioning their own assumptions even in some of their more impersonal novels. But with Conrad, it appears, only a tragic or intensely personal story or at least a very large one (such

as *Nostromo*) could induce these intellectual challenges
and self-scrutinies. Only a deep introspective drive, that
is, could disturb the smooth cluster of ideas on the surface. Such slight author-identification as exists in *The
Secret Agent* is clearly with the Assistant Commissioner –
especially when (tired of desk work) he leaves his office
to take a personal hand in the investigation and experiences a pleasing sense of loneliness and 'evil freedom'.
His life too is divided into an adventurous past and a
present of being chained to a desk. He is committed to
British respect for legality, order, liberty. But he knows
the excitement of the 'game' between policeman and outlaw. 'He stepped back into the full light of the room,
looking like the vision of a cool, reflective Don Quixote,
with the sunken eyes of a dark enthusiast and a very
deliberate manner.' This may well be the author in a
succinct if unconscious self-portrait. Yet the Assistant
Commissioner evokes none of the major emotional involvement and hence none of the profound intellectual
conflict we feel in the portrait of Razumov. The author's
relationship to the Assistant Commissioner is rational and
without uneasiness. Therefore he may be used to put,
clearly and unevasively, what the author has to say about
secret agents :

'No, Sir Ethelred. In principle, I should lay it down that the
existence of secret agents should not be tolerated, as tending
to augment the positive dangers of the evil against which
they are used. That the spy will fabricate his information
is a mere commonplace. But in the sphere of political and
revolutionary action, relying partly on violence, the professional spy has every facility to fabricate the very facts
themselves, and will spread the double evil of emulation
in one direction, and of panic, hasty legislation, unreflect-
ing hate on the other.'

This is clear expository dialogue, justified perhaps by Sir Ethelred's insistence on lucid simplicity. But it differs in no significant way from what Conrad might have said in an essay or letter to *The Times*. A more promising fictional situation occurs when the obsessed Professor pushes certain ideas of the author to a dangerous extreme, as in the discourse on the weak as a source of evil. This is a form of ironic self-evaluation Gide carried very far, but there is not much of it in *The Secret Agent*. More frequently the omniscient author *qua* author states his position unequivocally : tells us that revolutionists are 'the enemies of discipline and fatigue', or react fanatically to seeming injustice, or are guided by vanity, 'the mother of all noble and vile illusions, the companion of poets, reformers, charlatans, prophets, and incendiaries'. Significantly the Professor and the author-narrator sound very much alike when they make one of the novel's important points, that the terrorist and the policeman 'both come from the same basket'.

It is necessary to acknowledge, then, that *The Secret Agent* is not (so far as ideas are concerned) a work of exploration and discovery. It dramatizes positions already securely held and carries no farther than a casual essay might have. This short novel simply cannot be compared with *The Possessed* as a tragic study of moral anarchy and revolutionary psychology. But the ideas, once we have acknowledged the modesty of their pretentions, do contribute a great deal to the solidity and force of the entertainment. The asides on indolence, vanity, and so forth furnish footnotes to the continuing dramatized paradoxes : that the revolutionary or the double agent may be the laziest and most domesticated of bourgeois, that the policeman may have the mind of a criminal. The conservative assumptions concerning human nature, some of them to reappear in Graham Greene, were by no means banal in 1907, perhaps are not so today: that sympathy, 'which is a form of fear', may turn easily to rage and violence; that humanitarian and revolutionary ardors may derive from indolent egoism. The degenerate Stevie in his morbid horror of pain and in his indiscriminate compassion is a symbolic extreme both of the visionary and of his victim. The spectacle of a beaten horse (or dream of one, as in Dostoevsky) may be one cause of a crime.

This is not a tragic world of noble defeats and vast forces overthrown. *The Secret Agent*'s vision is of 'a mediocre mankind' in an 'imperfect society': flabby, debased, eternally gullible. The Stevies and other weaklings are always available, to be used and abused by the Verlocs and the Karl Yundts. 'With a more subtle intention, he [Yundt] took the part of an insolent and venomous evoker of sinister impulses which lurk in the blind envy and exasperated vanity of ignorance, in the suffering and misery of poverty, in all the hopeful and noble illusions of righteous anger, pity, and revolt.' And this poor humanity, whether we look to the left or to the counter-revolutionary right, is overcome by fatness as by a plague. It is the sign of a universal spiritual indolence. Michaelis the humanitarian idealist is 'oppressed by the layer of fat on his chest' and is round 'like a distended balloon'. Verloc has an 'air of having wallowed, fully dressed, all day on an unmade bed'; his 'vast bulk' offends his Embassy employers, who believe a pretended anarchist should be both unmarried and lean. Sir Ethelred the Secretary of State is also vast in bulk and stature, has a double chin, thick neck, and puffy lower lids. Even the blind terrorist of skinny hands, Karl Yundt, suffers from gouty swellings. The 'determined character' of Chief Inspector Heat's face is 'marred by too much flesh'.

Such then is Conrad's almost neo-Humanist view of revolutionary ardor, and his more personal view of

counterrevolutionary zeal; both views are unquestion-
ably sincere. It is most accurate, however, to look on them
as important parts of the 'entertainment', and to take the
vision of a monstrous town in the same light : this 'slimy
aquarium from which the water had run off', this 'immensity of greasy slime and damp plaster', this London. The rather gratuitous horror of the charwoman Mrs
Neale – 'aproned in coarse sacking up to the arm-pits' –
takes its place in an artistic composition of somber effects
as it could not, comfortably, in a more ambitious philosophical novel. The reader remains as coolly detached
from Mrs Neale, presumably, as from Stevie's wonderful
'steed of apocalyptic misery' whose lean thighs move 'with
ascetic deliberation'. The particular nature of Conrad's
'entertainment' is to hold the reader at a relatively fixed
distance of amused scorn from persons and situations
that, in an ordinary fiction, would evoke strong sentimental responses. Its prevailing tone is one of ironic
hauteur and control. The sum of so many instances of
calculated coldness may well be, as in Swift's 'Modest
Proposal', a serious and tenable compassion. But the
function of the irony, page by page, is to repudiate any
generous response to misfortune and disaster.

The Secret Agent is in several ways an astonishing
leap into an entirely different kind of art, and not least in
this absolute control of an ironic style operating in comparatively short and simple sentences. The style is elevated, but in the special sense of being elevated above the
miseries and squalors it describes; of remaining cool,
scornful, calculating, aloof. 'His prominent, heavy-lidded
eyes rolled sideways amorously and languidly, the bed-
clothes were pulled up to his chin, and his dark smooth
moustache covered his thick lips capable of much honeyed
banter.' This is almost the first glimpse of Mr Verloc.
And the detached style refuses to become excited or

compassionate at the moment of his death :

But they were not leisurely enough to allow Mr Verloc the time to move either hand or foot. The knife was already planted in his breast. It met no resistance on its way. Hazard has such accuracies. Into that plunging blow, delivered over the side of the couch, Mrs Verloc had put all the inheritance of her immemorial and obscure descent, the simply ferocity of the age of caverns, and the unbalanced nervous fury of the age of bar-rooms. Mr Verloc, the Secret Agent, turning slightly on his side with the force of the blow, expired without stirring a limb, in the muttered sound of the word 'Don't' by way of protest.

His body becomes, immediately, 'the mortal envelope of the late Mr Verloc reposing on the sofa', and Mrs Verloc the murderess becomes 'his widow'.

The particular chill humor of *The Secret Agent* derives from such elevation of passion and suffering to abstraction and from such reduction of the human being to a function or formal status. With each new use, the standard tags – Michaelis as the 'ticket-of-leave apostle' or Ossipon as 'nicknamed the Doctor' – become more denigrative. Karl Yundt ('the terrorist') is not just blind. He has 'extinguished eyes' in which an expression of 'underhand malevolence' survives. He is not an old and feeble man out for a walk, but a 'spectre' taking 'its constitutional crawl', helped by an 'indomitable snarling old witch'. Winnie Verloc contemplates with satisfaction the propriety of her respectable home, ensconced 'cosily behind the shop of doubtful wares'. 'Her devoted affection missed out of it her brother Stevie, now enjoying a damp villeggiatura in the Kentish lanes under the care of Mr Michaelis.' The word 'villeggiatura' is hardly one she would use or even know; it takes on the more ironic force because, as the reader knows and Winnie does not, Stevie was blown up that morning. On the same page Mr Verloc, who will very shortly be murdered, preserves an 'hieratic immobility' at the touch of an unexpected and lingering kiss. Comrade Ossipon's cold and scientific habit of speaking of Stevie as 'the degenerate' is less malicious than some of Conrad's linguistic modes. The merciless style marches ahead with an extraordinary assurance to its final view of Ossipon:

'I am seriously ill,' he muttered to himself with scientific insight. Already his robust form, with an Embassy's secret-service money (inherited from Mr Verloc) in his pockets, was marching in the gutter as if in training for the task of an inevitable future. Already he bowed his broad shoulders, his head of ambrosial locks, as if ready to receive the leather yoke of the sandwich board.

The great menaces to such a style are, of course, self-conscious coyness and polysyllabic humor; language, separating itself from an attitude to be expressed, may take pleasure in its own self-indulgence. But this almost never happens in *The Secret Agent*. We have instead a 'voice' which is an attitude, and which controls to an unusual degree its distance from the material. (Hence the two serious intrusions of a different authorial consciousness and voice, in the remarks on Alfred Wallace's book and on the Italian restaurant, are fairly startling.) In any event this controlled and relatively bare style did function for Conrad as a congenial point of view or narrating consciousness; style became, as it were, an interposed narrator. It satisfied the needs provided for in earlier novels by literal removal in time and space or by the screening Marlovian voice. As a result Conrad was able to carry through for almost the first time long dramatic scenes occurring in a fictional present; to achieve, even, excellent scenes of violent action, violent emotion, and violent comic discovery. *The Secret Agent* strongly contradicts our assumption (hitherto justified) that Conrad was least successful where he tried to do what most journeyman novelists can do. This is, in a way, his most 'professional' novel, and it appears that for this difference and for this new ease style, a deliberately cultivated new style, must be thanked or blamed. It provided him at all times with that historian's detachment he found so congenial. We have seen that Conrad could dramatize physical action and crisis so long as he imagined it occurring in the past. We now see he can dramatize such action and crisis in a fictional present, provided he sees it through scornful eyes that are not exactly his own. The style is a mask.

The professional ease and expertness show themselves in an almost flawless plotting: the events so contrived as to cause the characters a maximum discomfort, and to extract from the dramatized experience a maximum ironic significance. And the knowledge of these events withheld or offered in such a way as to make possible the greatest suspense and the most rewarding macabre comedy. It seems strange to speak of Conrad in these journalistic and conventional terms. But these are the terms that apply; the novel is an 'entertainment'. (The fifth chapter, in fact, is excellent detective fiction of a kind that would become very conventional.) Given the fact that this is a story of mystery and suspense, and that certain information must therefore be withheld, *The Secret Agent* makes things as easy as possible for its readers, and as grimly amusing. The reader is allowed to proceed through eighty straightforward pages before encountering a major interruption. Evidence may be concealed, but drama is not evaded. The satisfying discomfitures of Mr Vladimir and Mr Verloc and Comrade

Ossipon are dramatized not reported.

The 'surprises' are prepared with great care. The death of Stevie, which happens between the third and fourth chapters, is not formally revealed until near the end of the ninth; and the eighth chapter (a disguised flashback, which suggests Stevie is still alive) is certainly deceptive. Meanwhile enough clues have been dropped to make the final revelation seem inevitable and the death itself meaningful. From the beginning we have seen Stevie – the very type for Conrad of dumb, gullible, sentimental humanity – react neurotically to the overheard conversations of the anarchists. The death of Verloc, which he is to bring upon himself through the astonishing but overlong eleventh chapter, has been prepared from the end of the third. The 'funereal baked meats for Stevie's obsequies' are also for his own; the sharp carving knife and its possibilities were carefully hinted at almost two hundred pages before. The literary but still sinister business of putting out the light at the end of the third chapter virtually becomes, when repeated at the end of chapter eight, a sharp warning. The price of such total control is, of course, an occasional effect of contrivance. This realistic novel is by no means as true to life as the visionary impressionistic chiaroscuros, nor as conducive to serious psycho-moral involvement. But there is a certain pleasure to be derived from contemplation of the 'well made'. It is no paradox to say that this first 'entertainment' among Conrad's longer novels is also a very artful performance. Comedy is control.

The eleventh chapter (described by Leavis as 'one of the most astonishing triumphs of genius in fiction') is rich moral comedy, though it ends with the plunge of a knife. The misunderstanding is caused not by misinformation but by vanity, and Verloc rather than his wife takes the initiative in each important step toward his murder. For one of the first times we see Conrad extend a successful dramatic scene over many pages (too many, probably) and try to wring from it the last measure of drama, irony, meaning. The scene is too fully and too carefully explicated. However, it would be idle to quibble over such a fine and unexpected performance. I would simply propose that the twelfth chapter, and the farcical collision of Mrs Verloc and Comrade Ossipon, is an even greater success.

Here, to be sure, we have misinformation with a vengeance. The opportunistic Ossipon assumes that Verloc not Stevie was blown up in the Greenwich Observatory attempt, and now he is on his way to pay his respects to the widow. A discreet courtship of the money can come later. But she (terrified by the vision of being hanged 'amongst a lot of strange gentlemen in silk hats') is rushing away from her crime. They literally collide in the dark street. The astonished, scandalized, and presently terrified Ossipon hears Mrs Verloc abuse her husband's memory, profess interest in himself, suggest the police have already solved the bombing and that Verloc had connections with an Embassy. And beg him to save and hide her. But he does not understand that she is disjointedly confessing murder, and he must discover the body for himself. His final horror, as he learns that Winnie had killed her husband and that her brother 'the degenerate' had carried the bomb, is a scientific one. He gazes into her face like adamant 'as no lover ever gazed at his mistress's face. . . . He gazed at her, and invoked Lombroso, as an Italian peasant recommends himself to his favorite saint'. His remark to Winnie that the brother resembled her (which she interprets tenderly) presages his leap from the railway carriage. The macabre comedy is so successful, and Ossipon's growing horror and disgust so vivid, that it effectively destroys much of our sympathy for Winnie. We may come to share his view. But this is not too high a price to pay for such a show of fictional virtuosity.

For *The Secret Agent* is finally, and admirably, that: a work of virtuosity. This entertaining and easy book may well be the coldest and most restrained of Conrad's serious novels – a work so 'cold' that even some of his strongest preoccupations (such as the sense of isolation, such as the political conservativism) serve, chiefly, as materials for an ironic design.

SOURCE: *Conrad the Novelist* (1958) chap. 7, 'Two Versions of Anarchy', pp. 218–31.

Robert D. Spector

IRONY AS THEME:
CONRAD'S *THE SECRET AGENT*
(1958)

In his discussion of Conrad's *Secret Agent*, F. R. Leavis comments accurately upon the amazing unity of the work. At the same time, he recognizes that Conrad's irony 'is not a matter of an insistent and obvious "significance" of tone. . . .'[1] What the critic fails to note is that the basic structure of the novel is dependent upon its theme of irony, and his failure is a result of a misconception of the terms of irony that Conrad has brought to *The Secret Agent*.

Conrad himself speaks of his 'ironic treatment' of the subject.[2] In this instance, the proper function of the critic is to determine where the irony lies and what its significance is to the tale. Simply stated, *The Secret Agent* presents a perfect illustration of the ironic theme, cast in the characters of the story, and manifested in the plot.

West and Stallman have defined irony in terms that are fully appropriate to Conrad's novel :

Irony is based on contrast – between what seems to be intended and what is actually meant, between the apparent situation and the real one. In dramatic or tragic irony the spectator is aware of the ironic intent, of which the actor is ignorant. The spectator or reader knows the full situation of which the actors or characters, to the contrary, are ignorant.[3]

Such is the classical irony of *The Secret Agent*. Conrad's characters, certain in their knowledge of each other, actually are totally ignorant of the designs, plans, and thoughts of the people with whom they must deal, and of the way in which events *must* shape themselves.

Mrs Verloc fails to understand her mother's motives for leaving the Verloc household. In turn the mother cannot comprehend the reasons for her daughter's marriage, and both misjudge the actual character of the secret agent himself. They are as much responsible for Stevie's death as is Mr Verloc. Winnie's father-and-son vision of the pair permits her to ascribe all the wrong motives to Verloc's behavior and to insist silently upon a relationship that results in the death of her brother.

As for the secret agent, he is no more aware of his wife's feelings, thoughts, and motivation than she is of his. His destruction rests in his unquestioning acceptance of her assurance that Stevie will not get lost in following him; and in his misreading of her quietness, misjudgment of the depth of her passion for her brother, and unawareness of her capacity for action.

The death of Mrs Verloc, too, results from her misconception of the actual nature of Ossipon. What she sees as strength, the reader has already been invited to view as weakness. Ossipon – who should have had sufficient warning of her capacity for violence from the murder of her husband – is obtuse, fails to comprehend the motivation for her action, and consequently contributes to her suicide.

In connection with most of the minor characters as well, the theme of fatal ignorance governs the action. Conrad focuses upon the theme of his narrative by pointing out the Chief Inspector's assurance, just prior to Verloc's drastic crime, that there could not be anarchistic activity. Heat's discussion with the Assistant Commissioner offers again the portrait of two men making false evaluations of each other and of the situation, while acting upon the certainty of their limited views. Augmenting Heat's miscalculations is the Assistant Commissioner's conviction that it is safe to leave Verloc without a proper guard. Obviously, man works with perfect confidence in a world which moves without his knowledge.

Again in Ossipon's scenes with the Professor there is the same revelation of each man's ignorance of the other's knowledge. Upon their first meeting, Ossipon knows about the bombing, which the Professor does not – yet it is the Professor who has provided the materials for the anarchist plot. Then, at the conclusion of the novel, the Professor speaks 'knowingly' to Ossipon about matters of which the latter alone has intimate knowledge. Even in the final portrait of the Professor, Conrad spells out his theme: 'Nobody looked at him. He passed on unsuspected and deadly, like a pest in the street full of men.'

Leavis has actually come close to comprehending the theme of the novel, but without perceiving the importance of it to the structure and without realizing its significance:

The pattern of the book is contrived to make us feel the different actors or lives as insulated currents of feeling and purpose – insulated, but committed to co-existence and interaction in what they don't question to be a common world, and sometimes making disconcerting contacts through the insulation.[4]

Obviously, his final comment indicates that Leavis is unaware of the importance of the irony that is present in Conrad's deterministic theme, which fuses characterization and plot into an ultimate unity.

SOURCE: *Nineteenth-Century Fiction,* XIII (1958) 69–71.

NOTES

1. Leavis, *The Great Tradition*, p. 210.
2. *The Secret Agent*, p. xiii.
3. *The Art of Modern Fiction* (New York, 1949) p. 648.
4. Leavis, *The Great Tradition*, p. 210.

Avrom Fleishman

THE SYMBOLIC WORLD OF
THE SECRET AGENT (1965)

...... The two symbols, circle and triangle, may be considered to mark the poles of an axis on which the world of the novel revolves.[1] To review where we have come in this landscape of the symbolic world of *The Secret Agent*, the themes of secrecy, ignorance and madness describe a condition of social fragmentation which is Conrad's symbolic vision of the modern world and which is designated by the triangle. As we shall see, the enclosure and separateness of thin figures give rise to states of physical isolation, as well as to the mental isolation described above. Physical fragmentation is represented in the emphasis on the private life (including private property), in the environment of stone which surrounds the characters and to which they assimilate themselves, in the insularity which is prized in all realms of life, from dwelling-place to nation. The safety of physical isolation is, however, only an expedient and temporary one : its diseases are physical disorder, decay and explosion – just as 'madness and despair' were the diseases of mental isolation.

Physical disintegration begins in the tendency to reduce the human being to its component parts. Men are seen first as animals, then simply as fat, flesh, or meat. In this connection, the notion of cannibalism is introduced with telling effect. With the ultimate reduction of the human being to fragments of matter (' "He's all there. Every bit of him. It was a job" ' – p. 87), man is imaginatively

– and literally – annihilated in *The Secret Agent*. Conrad is the English writer who saw, as Brecht did, that in modern life 'man feeds on others'.

Closely related to the reduction of man to fragments is his reduction to inorganic matter :

. . . Mr Verloc, steady like a rock – a soft kind of rock – marched now along a street which could with every propriety be described as private. In its breadth, emptiness, and extent it had the majesty of inorganic nature, of matter that never dies. The only reminder of mortality was a doctor's brougham arrested in august solitude close to the curbstone. The polished knockers of the doors gleamed as far as the eye could reach, the clean windows shone with a dark opaque lustre. And all was still. But a milk cart rattled noisily across the distant perspective; a butcher boy, driving with the noble recklessness of a charioteer at Olympic Games, dashed round the corner sitting high above a pair of red wheels. A guilty-looking cat issuing from under the stones ran for a while in front of Mr Verloc, then dived into another basement; and a thick police constable, looking a stranger to every emotion, as if he, too, were part of inorganic nature, surging apparently out of a lamp-post, took not the slightest notice of Mr Verloc. (pp. 13–14)

This passage, at the approach of Verloc to the Embassy where the bomb-plot will be hatched, is based on the image of 'inorganic nature'. The street is broad, empty, extensive, even majestic – and it is alien to man. It is stone – 'matter that never dies'. Incapable of death, the world of inorganic nature is equally incapable of life, and the doctor's brougham enforces the associations of sickness and death. The brougham is 'arrested in august solitude close to the curbstone'; even a vehicle of motion becomes assimilated to the motionless and lonely world of stone. This inorganic world is not only of stone but of metal; the polished knockers gleaming 'as far as the eye could reach' evoke a wall of armor shutting out the human spectator and enclosing a realm of private property which does not emerge from behind its doors.

'And all was still.' With this masterly sentence, Conrad changes the pace of his prose and concludes the depiction of inorganic nature with its silence and immobility. At the same time he prepares for the eruption of vitality which will disturb the trance-like stillness of the street. For the butcher boy who next appears has a symbolic significance far beyond his peripheral place in the novel; 'driving with the noble recklessness of a charioteer at Olympic Games', he introduces the absent world of the vital and the human. The language of the sentence gives the mundane boy an heroic stature by its allusion to classical scenes of athletic glory. His reckless freedom is a style of life different from that of the holders of private property. (We remember that Winnie's romantic beau, whom she was forced to renounce because of economic necessity, was also a butcher-boy.) The other living beings in the street have, however, assimilated themselves to inorganic nature. The cat issues 'from under the stones' and quickly returns to a basement world of stone. The policeman appears to surge out of a lamp-post, takes no notice of the only other human present (Verloc), and seems a stranger to human emotion, 'as if he, too, were part of inorganic nature'.

The text following the passage quoted appears to be a gratuitous and somewhat frivolous divagation by Conrad on the subject of the irrationality of London streets and house numbers. It emerges, however, that the irrationality of the social order is crystallized in the confusion of the urban landscape. Its relation to the larger absurdities of society is suggested by Verloc's very acceptance of it: 'Mr Verloc did not trouble his head about it, his mission in life being the protection of the social mechanism, not its perfectionment or even its criticism' (p. 15). Verloc accepts this as he does other appearances of the absurd : by an impassivity which is itself absurd. Like the police constable surging out of the lamp-post, like the gleaming knockers on the exclusive doors, Verloc is opaque and inactive, having found his means of survival in the inhuman world by succeeding in some measure in turning himself into a rock – 'a soft kind of rock'. (Similarly, Mrs Verloc becomes petrified by the loss of her brother : the sound waves of Verloc's speech 'flowed around all the inanimate things in the room, lapped against Mrs Verloc's head as if it had been a head of stone' – p. 260.)

In addition to the inorganic, another realm of nature is employed by *The Secret Agent* to represent the non-human world – whatever is inimical to genuine social life. This other realm is the animal world, and its presence in man as physical animality – represented in the extreme case by gross fatness. In the interview at the Embassy, after Chancelier d'Embassade Wurmt has told Verloc that he is corpulent, Vladimir remarks to the latter, 'You are quite right, mon cher. He's fat – the animal' (p. 19). Men describe others as animals in this world quite as readily as they scorn them as fools, idiots or children. Even Conrad indulges in the tendency, when he describes Verloc as 'undemonstrative and burly in a fat-pig style' (p. 13). The imagery of the animal world acquires further symbolic force in the great chapter on the cab-ride of Winnie's mother to the old-age home. The cab-man's reflections on human misery are made manifest by the presence of the scruffy horse which draws them. When Stevie philosophizes with the equally scruffy cab-man on the theme, 'Bad world for poor people', he concludes with wide resonance, 'Beastly !' (p. 172). The imagery of ani-

mality reaches its crescendo in the pages following
Verloc's detection by Heat and the Assistant Commissioner, as he calls his nemesis, Vladimir, 'A Hyperborean
swine' (p. 212).

From this point on in the novel, allusions to animals
follow thick and fast. The Assistant Commissioner, before
reporting to the Great Personage – who is engaged in a
Parliamentary debate on a fisheries bill – passes the time
with the latter's secretary, 'Toodles', in an extended meta-
phoric allusion to the bomb-plot based on various sorts
of fishes. When Toodles inquires about the investigator's
'sprat', the latter answers that he has caught him, then
declares his intention of using Verloc as bait to catch a
'whale'. When Toodles inquires further, the Assistant
Commissioner characterizes the target, Vladimir, as a
'dog-fish'. 'It's a noxious, rascally-looking, altogether de-
testable beast, with a sort of smooth face and moustaches,'
says Toodles; his interlocutor tells him that his own
target is clean-shaven, 'a witty fish'. When told that the
dog-fish is a member of their own gentlemen's club,
Toodles sums up the conversation unwittingly by exclaim-
ing, 'That's the beastliest thing I've ever heard in my
life' (pp. 215–16).

Shortly thereafter, when the Assistant Commissioner
confronts Vladimir with his knowledge of the latter's
complicity in the bomb-plot, the metaphor shifts to dogs.
Vladimir calls Verloc, his accuser, 'a lying dog of some
sort', and the word enters the investigator's mouth:
'What pleased me most in this affair . . . is that it makes
such an excellent starting-point for a piece of work which
I've felt must be taken in hand – that is, the clearing out
of this country of all the foreign political spies, police,
and that sort of – of – dogs' (p. 226). To the Professor,
who is described in the last line of the novel as a 'pest in
the street full of men' (p. 311), the human community

seems, in turn, an animal existence: 'They swarmed numerous like locusts, industrious like ants, thoughtless like a natural force, pushing on blind and orderly and absorbed, impervious to sentiment, to logic, to terror, too, perhaps' (p. 82). The entire society comes to be seen as a jungle of animal forms obeying the laws of predatory survival. Alien to this world, forced to live in it yet inevitably devoured, men acquire the characters of beasts. The image of human animality is, when reduced to its lowest point, that of Mrs Neale, the Verlocs' charwoman: 'On all fours amongst the puddles, wet and begrimed, like a sort of amphibious and domestic animal living in ashbins and dirty water . . .' (p. 184).

Having reduced men to stones on the one hand and to pigs, dogs and fish on the other, *The Secret Agent* goes on to break them down into smaller components – into pieces of flesh or, potentially, meat. Verloc, regarding Stevie as a sort of domestic animal, is thereby made ready to employ him in a way that will reduce him further, to bits of flesh. Vladimir, in instructing Verloc in the 'philosophy of bomb-throwing', had disclaimed the intention of organizing 'a mere butchery' (p. 33), yet that is just what the event becomes: '. . . the Chief Inspector went on peering at the table with a calm face and the slightly anxious attention of an indigent customer bending over what may be called the by-products of a butcher's shop with a view to an inexpensive Sunday dinner' (p. 88). Despite his initial shock and revulsion, Heat's dispassion – the indifference of a trained investigator – is characteristic of a society that regards human beings as things, and can easily see them as mere meat when their bodies are reduced to fragments. These fragments are possible food for those who exploit the men they once were. Heat disdains these 'by-products of a butcher shop', but the remains of Stevie are compared to

the 'raw material for a cannibal feast' (p. 86). When
Verloc returns from his expedition, his wife places a cold
roast beef before him, 'examining the sharp edge of the
carving knife' as she sets it down (p. 193). After the visits
of the Assistant Commissioner and Heat indicate his game
is up, Verloc falls to eating again: 'The piece of roast
beef, laid out in the likeness of funereal baked meats for
Stevie's obsequies, offered itself largely to his notice. And
Mr Verloc again partook. He partook ravenously, without restraint and decency, cutting thick slices with the
sharp carving knife, and swallowing them without bread'
(p. 253). What Verloc is eating is the very flesh of Stevie:
the metaphor of a funeral banquet suggests Stevie's remains laid out on the table in the morgue. But Verloc
becomes mere meat in his turn: the carving knife with
which he savagely cuts the beef will shortly become the
instrument of his wife's revenge. Then Verloc himself
will be fragmented: the shadow of his corpse, his blood
dripping like the ticking of a clock, his hat 'rocking slightly
on its crown' in the middle of the floor – all the images of
the dead are of dismemberment into organic flesh or inorganic things. Finally, his blood forms a 'beastly pool'
around his solitary hat, both separated from his human
body (p. 287).

The imagery of cannibalism is in accord with anarchist
doctrine. It is Karl Yundt, the most repulsive of the sham
revolutionaries, who suggests this vision of modern
society: 'Do you know how I would call the nature of the
present economic conditions? I would call it cannibalistic.
That's what it is! They are nourishing their greed on the
quivering flesh and the warm blood of the people –
nothing else' (p. 51). Coming in this form, the image
seems an exaggeration and a piece of anarchist lunacy.
The novel proves it to be an accurate description of the
workings of society. In this condition men are dis-

membered not only accidentally or metaphorically but systematically – as in the novel's report of the German recruits whose ears are torn off by their officers. It is this condition that Stevie wishes to rectify; he had seized the avenging carving knife and 'would have stuck that officer like a pig if he had seen him then' (p. 60). It is, however, for him to be dismembered and for his sister to stick his porcine destroyer dead.

The ultimate reduction of man, even beyond fragmentation into flesh and transformation into matter, is his total annihilation. The death of Verloc brings on the same kind of crescendo of 'nothing' as occurs in *King Lear*:

Nothing brings them [the dead] back, neither love nor hate. They can do nothing to you. They are as nothing. . . . now he was of no account in every respect. He was of less practical account than the clothing on his body, than his overcoat, than his boots – than that hat lying on the floor. He was nothing. . . . [he] was less than nothing now. . . . (pp. 266–7)

This metaphor of the nothingness of man was made literal on a mass scale in recent history. On this basis, we are prepared to see Winnie's incoherent muttering – 'Blood and dirt. Blood and dirt.' (p. 290) – not only as a reflection on the state to which her brother has been reduced, but as a vision of the course of human history. It is this vision which stands behind the Professor's statement that '. . . blood alone puts a seal on greatness. . . . Blood. Death. Look at history' (p. 304). . . .

SOURCE : *English Literary History*, xxxii (1965) 205–11.

NOTE

1. [Editor's Note.] The article citied is on pp. 196–219 of *ELH*, xxxii (1965). The excerpt above is section ii, 'The Physical World', pp. 205–11. The first section deals with 'The Moral World', and the third with 'Space and Time'.

J. Hillis Miller

FROM *POETS OF REALITY* (1965)

And in those days shall men seek death, and shall not find it;
and shall desire to die, and death shall flee from them.

(Revelation 9 : 6)

In *The Secret Agent* Conrad's voice and the voice of the
darkness most nearly become one.[1] To explore the meaning of this novel will be to approach as close as possible
to the dark heart of Conrad's universe. Its starting place
is a certain conception of modern society. Against this
background the events of what Conrad, in his dedication
to H. G. Wells, calls 'This Simple Tale of the XIX Century' (p. v), enact themselves. Apparently Conrad's
notion of modern society is the one implied by the germ
idea of the story. That germ was a discussion of anarchist
activities, particularly of 'the already old story of the
attempt to blow up the Greenwich Observatory; a bloodstained inanity of so fatuous a kind that it was impossible
to fathom its origin by any reasonable or even unreason-
able process of thought' (p. x). Conrad's attitude is not
merely one of 'pity and contempt' for the 'criminal futility' of anarchism, 'doctrine, action, mentality', mixed with
'indignation' (pp. viii, ix) deriving from his sense of the
threat the anarchists pose to a good society kept stable by
fidelity to duty. Conrad is not a conservative of this sort
at all. . . . The vision of society which informs *The Secret
Agent* is not that of a stable civilization threatened by the
absurd criminality of a lot of 'half-crazy' (p. ix) anarchists.

Conrad sees all society as rotten at the core, as a vast half-deliberate conspiracy of police, thieves, anarchists, tradesmen, aristocratic blue-stockings, minister of state, and ambassadors of foreign powers.

Conrad's symbol for this web of secret connections is London itself, the enormous commercial and industrial city. Within the city everyone is related to everyone else, often in hidden and unlawful ways, and at the same time each person is cut off from his neighbors in a solitude 'as lonely and unsafe as though [he] had been situated in the midst of a forest' (p. 201). . . .

The city is the place imposing the mode of human relationship peculiar to modern life. It is also 'man-made', a monstrous human construction which surrounds man with his own image, and hides from him the light and truth of nature. The city generates its own darkness, an especially human one, not the transhuman blackness of *Heart of Darkness*, but an obscurity made of illusion, fatuity, and blindness, the blindness of five million people who agree, with Winnie Verloc, that 'life doesn't stand much looking into' (p. xiii).

Enclosed within this comfortable darkness, all men – anarchist, policeman, tradesman, and thief – accept certain assumptions. They agree that life is a game with rules everyone must obey, that many of these conventions cannot be talked about openly, and that nothing must be done to upset the delicate balance between thief and policeman, anarchist and reactionary ambassador. All of these classes of men deny their co-operation with the others. All are more or less consciously living a lie. They are alike in their refusal to look for the truth behind the surface of things, and in their determination to maintain the status quo. Like Winnie Verloc, they waste 'no portion of this transient life in seeking for fundamental information' (p. 169). Their instinct is not to question

themselves or the world, but to be and let be. They remain
as little conscious as possible, and as much as possible
bound by unthinking habits. Chief Inspector Heat, forced
to deal with anarchists, regrets 'the world of thieves —
sane, without morbid ideals, working by routine, respectful of constituted authorities, free from all taint of hate
and despair' (pp. 92, 93): 'he could understand the
mind of a burglar, because, as a matter of fact, the mind
and the instincts of a burglar are of the same kind as the
mind and the instincts of a police officer. Both recognize
the same conventions, and have a working knowledge of
each other's methods and of the routine of their respective
trades. . . . Products of the same machine, . . . they take
the machine for granted in different ways, but with a
seriousness essentially the same' (p. 92). Society is a
machine, a man-made system of conventions obeyed as
much by thief as by policeman. The man-made machine
has ended by making men, and by determining their
existence within a framework of which many of them are
not aware and which they do not wish to question. . . .
It is the Professor who most explicitly identifies the attitude of the revolutionists with that of respectable people.
'You revolutionists', he says, 'are the slaves of the social
convention, which is afraid of you; slaves of it as much as
the very police that stands up in the defence of that convention. Clearly you are, since you want to revolutionize
it. . . . You plan the future, you lose yourselves in reveries
of economical systems derived from what is; whereas
what's wanted is a clean sweep and a clear start for a new
conception of life' (pp. 69, 73).

A clean sweep and a clear start — the only hope would
be to escape altogether from the darkness of the city, but
this would be possible only through the 'destruction of
what is' (p. 306). All ways of living short of that are the
same, whether they seek to maintain things exactly as

they are, or whether, like the Marxism of Michaelis, they foresee an inevitable development, governed by the material laws of production, from the present state of things to a better one in the future. Anything derived from what is could only be a rearrangement of elements which suffer from a fatal weakness. They are a human creation, as tools, as money, as laws, as the bricks and stones of the city are shaped by man and therefore without authenticity. Conrad . . . sees civilization as an arbitrary creation, resting on no source of value outside human-ity. His picture of the sinister cooperation of policemen, anarchists, and ministers of state within the brooding darkness of the enormous town is one of his most impres-sive dramatizations of this black view of civilized society.

Only if man were in some way liberated from the dark-ness could he be freed from his fatuous complacency. The purpose of the novel is to bring about such a libera-tion for the reader by effecting it for the chief characters of the novel, and the objects of Conrad's 'inspiring in-dignation and underlying pity and contempt' are not only the revolutionists of the story, but all men, his readers too, trapped, like the characters of the story, in a blind belief in what is a human fabrication and a lie.

Since *The Secret Agent* is a work of literature, its power to liberate the reader from his infatuation must derive from a certain use of words. Since it is a novel, words must be used in it to describe the appearances of an imagined scene, and to dramatize human actions within that scene. What the scene is we know : the enormous town, genera-tor of its own darkness and devourer of the world's light. To describe this town from the point of view of someone blindly enclosed in it would be no way out of the darkness. The nature of the collective dream is invisible to the dreamers because it determines what is seen and how it is judged. If society is to be exposed there must be a withdrawal to some vantage point outside it. Some dreamers must waken and be able to compare the waking world to the dream.

Conrad chooses two ways of separating his readers from the dark city. The first of these is the point of view of the narrator. His stance is one of ironic detachment. The 'purely artistic purpose' of the novel, Conrad says, is 'that of applying an ironic method to a subject of that kind' (p. xiii). The detachment of an ironic perspective is necessary because the clear vision of an uninvolved spectator is the mode of seeing of the waking sleeper, the man who knows all he sees is permeated by the unreality of dreams. Such a man is both inside and outside his dream at once, and can describe it with meticulous precision, while knowing that it is a dream. . . .

Conrad wants to do more than show the dream as dream. He also wants to show what is outside it, to reveal the light which is swallowed up by the city's darkness. . . . Conrad must therefore use another method of separating his readers from the urban dream. He must show characters whose enclosure in the dream is destroyed. Only because such people exist in the novel can the narrator describe not only the dream, but what the dream hides.

The plot of *The Secret Agent* is a chain reaction, a sequence of disenchantments started by M. Vladimir's demand that Verloc create a sensational anarchist demonstration. The chain leads from Verloc eventually to Winnie Verloc, and then to the man who survives her and must live on with the terrible knowledge of her death, Comrade Ossipon. One by one these characters are wrested from their complacency and put in a situation which is outside everything they have known, a situation which is, one might say, out of this world. Conrad's ways of describing these cataclysmic experiences are necessarily hyperbolic. Winnie Verloc, after she learns of Stevie's death, is a 'free woman'. Her freedom is of such a terrifying completeness that she cannot see 'what there [is] to keep her in the world at all' (p. 251). Her 'moral nature' has been 'subjected to a shock of which, in the physical order, the most violent earthquake of history could only be a faint and languid rendering' (p. 255). Similar shocks destroy the unthinking insulation of other characters. Winnie is the central figure only because she goes from the most complete innocence to the most shattering knowledge of what lies beyond the world. . . .

A narrator who sees the story with clearheaded pity and contempt, and characters who move toward this detachment – these are the two modes of vision which Conrad uses to 'make us *see*' the conditions of life in the city.

When the comfortable dream of a humanized world is rudely shattered, man sees what has been there all along. Reality is always present, but is usually hidden behind the façade of meanings which has been spread over the world. Through the detachment of the ironic narrator and through the experience of the characters the reader is brought to see this dissimulated reality. Such seeing takes several forms, each corresponding to a stage of penetration into reality.

All the levels of this penetration are unobtrusively introduced in an admirable passage at the beginning of the second chapter. This text describes the progress of Mr Verloc through the streets of London as he walks one spring morning toward the embassy which houses one of his employers:

The very pavement under Mr Verloc's feet had an old-gold tinge in that diffused light, in which neither wall, nor tree, nor beast, nor man cast a shadow. Mr Verloc was going westward through a town without shadows in an atmosphere of powdered old gold. There were red, coppery gleams on the roofs of houses, on the corners of walls, on the panels of carriages, on the very coats of the horses, and on the broad back of Mr Verloc's overcoat, where they produced a dull effect of rustiness. . . . The polished knockers of the doors gleamed as far as the eye could reach, the clean windows shone with a dark opaque lustre. And all was still. But a milk cart rattled noisily across the distant perspective; a butcher boy, driving with the noble recklessness of a charioteer at Olympic Games, dashed round the corner sitting high above a pair of red wheels. . . . (pp. 11–12)

Conrad has here made use of the fact that weather of a particular sort brings about a startling transformation of the usual look of things. The diffused light makes everything look alien. Instead of seeing houses, walls, carriages, and people as distinct objects, the spectator also sees the identical gleams which the diffused light casts on each indiscriminately. It may be, in fact, that nothing exists except these gleams, since one evidence of the solidity of objects, the fact that they interrupt the light and cast shadows, is missing. No thing or person has a shadow, and it is as if they did not exist as massive forms, but had been dissolved into scintillations of light. To see things in this way is to understand how little of what is seen derives from objects themselves, and how much is a reflection of the pervasive light which makes things visible. The spectator sees that the world is composed of splotches and blobs and gleams, gleams which his intelligence distorts by fitting them into its pre-existent concepts. . . . . . .

In this passage, as elsewhere in *The Secret Agent*, the spectator comes to see how familiar objects exceed the

mind's grasp and dwell beyond human meanings. The
milk cart and the butcher boy's chariot which appear
before Mr Verloc's eyes have no connection with each
other, and no special meaning for Mr Verloc. They
appear one after the other against the drab background
of the silent street, and are followed by 'a guilty-looking
cat issuing from under the stones', and a 'thick police
constable' who surges 'apparently out of a lamp-post'
(p. 14). These objects exist with three-dimensional solidity between the spectator and the veil of light which
forms the background of the scene. They can be identified, but nothing more can be said of them. Recognitions
of the intrinsic absurdity of things most often occur in
moments of violence, danger, or surprise, times when
man's ordinary engagement in the world is broken. Such
moments occur in *The Secret Agent* when Verloc's
complacent life is endangered by M. Vladimir, and when
the reader first hears of the violent death of Stevie:

He was, in truth, startled and alarmed. . . . And in the
silence Mr Verloc heard against a window-pane the faint
buzzing of a fly – his first fly of the year. . . . The useless
fussing of that tiny, energetic organism affected unpleas-
antly this big man threatened in his indolence. (pp. 26, 27)

An upright semi-grand piano near the door, flanked by
two palms in pots, executed suddenly all by itself a valse
tune with aggressive virtuosity. The din it raised was deaf-
ening. [Then] it ceased, as abruptly as it had started. . . .
(p. 6)

Apparently the shapes and colors of things, their appearance as mute presences, have a quality of firstness before
which it is impossible to go. Behind the visible qualities
of things, however, is something else: the substance of
which they are made. Behind the gleams of colors or light

as Mr Verloc makes his way through the street, behind the houses, walls, carriages, and trees which these gleams reveal and hide, is 'the majesty of inorganic nature, of matter that never dies' (p. 14). All things have this in common : they are made of immortal matter. This may be more important, in determining each thing, than the fact that one particular bit of matter has been given just this shape or structure. Repeatedly in *The Secret Agent* Conrad reminds the reader that the forms which man imposes on matter effect only a precarious transformation. At any moment a change in his way of looking at things or a change in the things themselves will force him to see the reality behind surface colors or shapes. This chthonic substance is prior to what had seemed irreducible qualities and is far more alien to man than they. . . . . . . The 'majesty of inorganic nature' appears in the solidity, immobility, and inertia of matter. Whatever may be done to it, it remains fundamentally the same. It is outside time, since time cannot change it, and it transcends all attempts to understand or control it. Matter is static and perdurable, and therefore alien to man, that creature of time and change.

Man in one way participates in the majesty of matter that never dies. Though his body is organic rather than inorganic, it comes from matter and returns to it. Even while a man is alive his body is as inertly passive as are rocks and bricks. Mr Verloc marches along the street 'steady like a rock – a soft kind of rock' (p. 13), and the thick police constable surges out of a lamp-post 'as if he, too, were part of inorganic nature' (p. 14). From the point of view of consciousness, the fact that men are in one sense part of nature is the most shocking evidence of the strangeness of matter. If a man exceeds his body by reason of his knowledge, his intentions, memories, and thoughts, in another way he is trapped in his body. He is just this piece of matter here, so many pounds of flesh and blood, like a soft rock, and, like a rock, enclosed within his own bounds. Ordinarily the grossness, or, one might say, the obscenity of a man's enclosure in a thick envelope of flesh is not noticed, so powerful are the evidences of his spirituality, but fat men remind us of the scandal of our incarnation, just as does the sight of a corpse. It is this fact as much as the evidence it gives of gluttony which, it may be, makes obesity seem morally wrong. A fat man seems in danger of ceasing to have a soul and becoming simply a body, and this recalls the grotesque absurdity of our own incarnation. Mr Verloc can more justly be called 'a soft kind of rock' because he is fat than if he were thin. He is 'undemonstrative and burly in a fat-pig style' (p. 13), and the police constable who looks as if he had just surged out of a lamp-post is 'thick'.

With something of a shock the reader realizes how many of the characters in *The Secret Agent* are fat. Conrad seems to be insisting on their gross bodies, as if their fatness were connected with the central themes of the novel. . . .

A clue to the reason why there are so many fat characters in *The Secret Agent* is given by what happens to Stevie, one of the few characters who is not fat. Stevie is blown to bits when he stumbles with a can of explosives on his way to destroy the Greenwich Observatory. The disappearance of this half-witted boy is the central event of the novel, but it is never directly described. Stevie's end is hinted at, imagined, and approached from various perspectives. It is recounted by various people, but remains hidden, a blank place in the center of the narrative. Stevie's death is proof that human beings are radically different from the majesty of matter that never dies. . . .

Stevie is dead, but in another sense he is not dead at all. Conrad insists on this other sense. He returns to it, and broods over it, as though it were an important fact in the story. Stevie is not annihilated. He is transformed into 'a heap of rags, scorched and bloodstained, half concealing what might have been an accumulation of raw material for a cannibal feast' (p. 86). He is 'blown to small bits : limbs, gravel, clothing, bones, splinters – all mixed up together' (p. 210). He becomes 'a heap of nameless fragments', like 'the by-products of a butcher's shop' (pp. 87, 88). Stevie's death is shocking proof of man's incarnation. It proves that a man cannot, even after death, escape from his identification with so many pounds of inorganic nature that never dies. When Stevie dies his consciousness vanishes, but he does not leave a vacuum behind him. He leaves an 'enormous hole in the ground under a tree filled with smashed roots and broken branches. All round fragments of a man's body blown to pieces' (p. 70).

Man's identification with his body has another meaning for Conrad. This meaning is dramatized in the character of the Professor. 'Exterminate, exterminate !' he says, echoing the note at the bottom of Kurtz's pamphlet in *Heart of Darkness*. 'That is the only way of progress. . . . Every taint, every vice, every prejudice, every convention must meet its doom' (p. 303). For this reason he gives explosives to anyone who asks for them. 'The condemned social order', as the Professor says, 'has not been built up on paper and ink, and I don't fancy that a combination of paper and ink will ever put an end to it' (p. 71). Though the social edifice is made up of a vast system of institutions based on an 'idealistic conception of legality' (p. 73), nevertheless these intangible ideals have got themselves embodied in a very tangible form. They exist not only in the bricks and stones of London, but also in the stolid inertia of the citizens of London, shopkeepers, lazy, fat revolutionists, and 'thick' police-

men alike. Incarnation means more than the imprisonment of spirit in a body. It also means the imprisonment
of spirit within the narrow bounds of a set of imperfect
assumptions about law and morality. For this reason the
Professor's bombs must destroy more than the buildings
of modern civilization. They must destroy people too, for
in them history is embodied as much as in stones and in-
scriptions. . . .

The Professor fails. He remains poised indefinitely
in the moment between the discovery of his sinister freedom and the act which would use that freedom to liberate mankind. . . . The Professor's failure is strikingly sym-
bolized in his search for a perfect detonator, and in the
bomb which he carries on his own person as the expression of his 'force of personality' (p. 67). Rather than
be captured, he will press the india-rubber ball in his
pocket and blow himself and those around him to bits.
The only flaw in this 'supreme guarantee of his sinister
freedom' (p. 81) is the full twenty seconds which must
elapse from the moment he presses the detonator until
the explosion takes place. The failure of the detonator
expresses the contradiction which keeps the Professor
hovering interminably in the infinite moment between
the decision to bring about the 'destruction of what is'
and the moment of the explosion. Death is too powerful
to be used as an instrument. It is always an end, in more
senses than one. The man who tries to bring death into
the human world as a means of purification will find that
he has committed the world to death. He cannot destroy
men's beliefs without actually killing them. To perform
such a delicate operation of purification would require
infinite time, whereas the Professor's time is finite. One
slip, one tiny error, and, instead of bringing death into
the world, he will send that world, or part of it, into eternity, and eternity, as Ossipon says, is 'a damned hole'.

'It's time that you need. You – if you met a man who could give you for certain ten years of time, you would call him your master. . . . Wait till you are lying flat on your back at the end of your time. . . . Your scurvy, shabby, mangy little bit of time' (pp. 305, 306). Time, in Ossipon's speech, is opposed to eternity, in a juxta-position which recurs throughout the novel. Time can be measured by man, as it is in the Greenwich Observatory. It can be employed as a dimension within which man fulfills his intentions. Eternity, the realm of death, is a damned hole, of no use to man. The imperfection of the Professor's detonator is a symptom of his inability to re-concile time and eternity.

His failure can be defined in another way. He cannot make a large enough blank place to bring into existence his new conception of life. His bombs are not big enough to make a clean sweep. Mankind is 'as numerous as the sands of the seashore, as indestructible, as difficult to handle', and the sound of exploding bombs will be 'lost in their immensity of passive grains without an echo' (p. 306). Only if the Professor could destroy mankind at the same moment as he killed himself would he be justi-fied in pressing the india-rubber ball. A vacuum less than total will still leave some men tied to history, believing in the old conventions and laws, and ready to continue the old rather than to initiate the new. The Professor's bombs are too weak, and this weakness alone keeps him from suicide.

The impasse of the Professor explains Conrad's insis-tence that an explosion does not leave a vacuum but what was there before in a different form. The indestructibil-ity of inorganic nature is identified with the stolid obduracy of human personality. The 'constitutional in-dolence' (p. 169) of so many of the characters in the novel is the exact moral correlative of their obesity. People insist on being themselves in the same way that a grain of sand resists destruction, and the world is dominated by a law of individuality. Each thing or person is just the thing or person it is and no other. This habit of self-hood resists the Professor's attempts to return it to anonymity in order to make a new start. . . . 'Often while walking abroad, when he happened also to come out of himself, he had such moments of dreadful and sane distrust of mankind. What if nothing could move them?' (pp. 81, 82).

'Often while walking abroad' – the Professor's suspicion that nothing can move mankind comes when he himself is moving. To be outside the refuge of his room, that 'hermitage of the perfect anarchist' (p. 82), is to be in danger of recognizing 'the resisting power of numbers, the unattackable stolidity of a great multitude' (p. 95). It is to be in danger of seeing the heavy weight of history as it is embodied in the present. This happens only occasionally, when the Professor happens to come out of himself as well as out of his room. It is possible for him to go through the streets in complete separation from the surrounding world, as when he walks 'with the nerveless gait of a tramp going on, still going on, indifferent to rain or sun in a sinister detachment from the aspects of sky and earth'. . . . (p. 96)

The effect of motion on an inorganic mass exactly parallels the effect of the presence of mind within a human body. A body inhabited by consciousness is freed from its materiality and seems detached from the surrounding world, just as a man who is walking seems more alive than a motionless one. John Hagan, Jr, has shown the importance of the motif of the interview in *The Secret Agent*.[2] Equally important is the image of walking. It expresses a 'sinister freedom' rather than attempts at communication. Verloc, the Professor, the

Assistant Commissioner, Inspector Heat, Winnie Verloc, and Comrade Ossipon are at different times shown walking through the streets of London, and an entire chapter is given to an apparently irrelevant description of a journey by cab to the poor-house. The purpose of this extraordinary chapter is to create a dreamlike atmosphere dramatizing the paradox of man's ability to move himself through the world and thereby escape from it. . . .

The theme of *The Secret Agent* seems to be the disjunction between matter and spirit. Matter is solid and resists change. It never dies. Spirit, on the other hand, dwells in time. It moves across matter without being bound by it. Spirit is free. Man lives in both realms. He is incarnated in a body and is therefore part of matter which never dies. He also has a mind. The two dimensions of his existence are incompatible. He can neither incarnate spirit in matter, nor can he immaterialize matter until it takes on the quality of spirit. The gross weight of earth lies untouched behind the façade of the city, and the human mind which created that façade is as fleeting as ever. Man always dies in the end. Conrad's vision seems to culminate in the recognition of an irreconcilable dualism. Man is the meeting place of matter and spirit, and he is riven apart by their contradictions.

Such a notion of the human situation would have at least two consolations. Though man's mind is emptiness and negation, this negation is a power. It is the basis of the changes which have produced civilization. Cities have, after all, been made with stones and bricks. Even though the brute substance of their matter may not have been altered, they have been shaped to man's uses. Society, though it may be based on a lie, still works, as long as everyone agrees to accept the lie as truth. Men have the power to create a vast system based on an 'as if'. This

system is almost as good as if it were real, so effectively
has truth been hidden away by the film which man has
spread over the world. Though Conrad reveals the
factitiousness of human society, he also presents it as a
creation which has a pragmatic validity. . . .

Conrad's view of human life apparently depends on
two notions of nothingness, the nothingness of consciousness, and the nothingness of death, and these support his
despair and his hope. If society is based on the creative
power of man's mind it is based on nothing. If death
is nothingness too, it is harmless, and man is free to make
of his own nothingness what he will. He can make with
impunity an earthly city of man. . . .

Of the three deaths in *The Secret Agent*, those of Stevie,
Verloc, and Winnie, only one is described directly, Winnie's murder of Verloc, but in the latter case as in the
others the emphasis is not on death as escape into
nothingness. The focus is rather on the experience of
someone who survives the death of another as if it had
been his own death and remains behind as a kind of walking corpse. The survivor is transported into a horrible
realm where every place is no place, and where time
moves without getting anywhere. This metamorphosis is
a process of depersonalization. It follows on the break-
down of the ordinary habits linking a person to the sanity
of the everyday world. A man ceases to be the person he
was, tied by a hundred strands to an enduring role in
society, and becomes nobody, an anonymous awareness
or wakefulness which cannot be called a self. The horror
of this state is the way it suggests that it may be impossible
to die. A man who reaches it is still alive, though everything about him is dead. Everything which had defined
him as himself is gone, and yet, terrifyingly, he is still
there. Only the language of exaggeration will do to des-

cribe this condition. After Winnie has killed her husband she becomes 'a woman enjoying her complete irresponsibility and endless leisure, almost in the manner of a corpse' (p. 263), and the Assistant Commissioner says of Verloc after the death of Stevie: 'It sounds an extravagant way of putting it, . . . but his state of dismay suggested to me an impulsive man who, after committing suicide with the notion that it would end all his troubles, had discovered that it did nothing of the kind' (p. 220).

To be in Verloc's state or Winnie's, is to be unable to die and yet unable to return to life. It is to persist in an interminable moment of freedom, irresponsibility, and leisure. This moment has no content. It is free of everything. Winnie does not 'think at all' (p. 263). Yet it is not nothing. It is a positive awareness of nothing. Such a state of mind is, in Conrad's precise words, 'madness or despair'. It is a living death whose horror is its inability to escape from itself.

The most frightful aspect of this state is the fact that chaos and eternity are not set against man as something he sees from the outside. They are inside, waiting for an opportunity to appear at the surface and engulf him. Mr Verloc, after M. Vladimir has shattered his enclosure in the routine of his ambiguous existence, is unable to sleep. He is denied that daily oblivion which is a rehearsal of death and an expression of a man's unthinking commitment to his life. Verloc's insomnia anticipates not the forgetfulness of sweet death, but Winnie's terrifying freedom, the freedom of a living corpse. . . . . . .

To leave the surface levels of the mind and be merged in the night like a statue in the rough is not to lose consciousness or die. Winnie remains very much alive. She survives Stevie's death, which cuts her sole tie to the world, and lives on to drink her 'cup of horrors' (p. 298) to the last drop. The emphasis in this section of the novel

is not on the death of Verloc, but on Winnie and the extraordinary state of mind she reaches. This state is described in an accumulation of details which shows her
progressively approaching a state of anonymity and melt-
ing into the blackness of death. Her state is like that of a
somnambulist or insomniac. She is awake. She watches
with a lucid vigilance, but she does not watch anything.
She looks at a blank wall: '[Mr Verloc] was startled by
the inappropriate character of his wife's stare. It was not
a wild stare, and it was not inattentive, but its attention
was peculiar and not satisfactory, inasmuch that it seemed
concentrated upon some point beyond Mr Verloc's person. The impression was so strong that Mr Verloc glanced
over his shoulder. There was nothing behind him: there
was just the whitewashed wall. . . . Mrs Verloc gazed at
the whitewashed wall. A blank wall – perfectly blank.
A blankness to run at and dash your head against.'
(pp. 239, 240, 244.) Everything Winnie sees has been
turned into another expression of death. If what she sees
is a symbol of death, she also contains death within herself. This inner death is a bottomless pool which reduces
to its own blackness everything she looks at, even the light
itself: '[Mr Verloc] looked straight into his wife's eyes.
The enlarged pupils of the woman received his stare
into their unfathomable depths.' (p. 248); A tinge of
wildness in her aspect was derived . . . from the fixity of
her black gaze where the light of the room was absorbed
and lost without the trace of a single gleam.' (p. 259.)

Winnie's depersonalization goes on through the sequence of events leading from her discovery that Verloc
has caused Stevie's death to her murder of her husband,
her meeting with Comrade Ossipon, their return to the
shop, and his abandonment of her on the train going toward the Channel boat from which she will leap at last
into the dark water. The sea is another expression of the

presence which lies behind or within every form and person, and Winnie's suicide is the physical fulfillment of the state she has already reached in her mind. Conrad can say of her that, even while she was alive, when she spoke 'it was as if a corpse had spoken' (p. 247), and that 'she was not deadly. She was death itself – the companion of life.' (p. 291.) Winnie lives on in the endless tossing of the waves and in Ossipon's awareness of how she had died, just as, when she kills Verloc, Stevie is resurrected in her, 'as if the homeless soul of Stevie had flown for shelter straight to the breast of his sister, guardian, and protector' (p. 262).

Poor Comrade Ossipon, the unwilling accomplice of Winnie, is the last survivor of the chain reaction which began with M. Vladimir's shattering of Verloc's complacency. He survives to become the inheritor of the terrible knowledge which has destroyed Verloc and Winnie, and to enter a state of living death in which, walking, he does not get anywhere, and in which he finds it impossible to sleep :

He could walk. He walked. He crossed the bridge. . . . And again Comrade Ossipon walked. His robust form was seen that night in distant parts of the enormous town slumbering monstrously on a carpet of mud under a veil of raw mist. . . . He walked through Squares, Places, Ovals, Commons, through monotonous streets with unknown names where the dust of humanity settles inert and hopeless out of the stream of life. He walked . . . (pp. 300, 301)

The conjunction here of the motifs of walking and insomnia reveals the meaning of each. Walking does not express the freedom of spirit, its ability to skim over the surface of things and break away from the changelessness of matter. It signifies man's inability to escape from himself. Like insomnia, it corresponds to a state of mind which is contradictory or impossible, and yet real. Much earlier in the novel, Verloc's 'dreary conviction that there was no sleep for him', his 'mute and hopelessly inert . . . fear of darkness' (p. 60), is expressed in the sound of footsteps in the street below his bedroom window: 'Down below in the quiet, narrow street measured footsteps approached the house, then died away, unhurried and firm, as if the passer-by had started to pace out all eternity, from gas-lamp to gas-lamp in a night without end.' (p. 57.) Insomnia is like a walking which begins nowhere and goes nowhere, but moves for ever without advancing, always at the same distance from an infinitely distant starting place and an infinitely far-off goal, like the endless ticking of the Verlocs' clock on the staircase. Insomnia puts a man within a time which has not started from any remembered beginning and does not go toward any end. Time passes, but the insomniac can no longer remember when he first lay down to sleep, nor can he anticipate the morning. He seems to have left all that behind him for good. Each moment exactly repeats the other, with the same emptiness, and the same disconnection from anything before or after. The most horrible part of the insomniac's suffering is his sense that his unwinking wakefulness will persist for ever in a night without end, an eternal vigilance without object. The clock's steady tick, measure of human time, melts into eternity, just as the dropping of Verloc's blood, which Winnie confounds with the sound of the clock, first accelerates and then becomes a steady flow as he dies. Walking expresses spatially what sleeplessness expresses temporally. Like insomniacs, walkers can move interminably without escaping from themselves. The city is a labyrinth of streets in which a man may go from place to place without getting anywhere, for each place is the same as all the other places.

Far from proving the independence of the mind, walking shows how man, living in time and change, possesses death not as the end of his life, but as the substance of his present state.

The social fiction of laws, conventions, ideals, and personalities exists in the past and in the future, never in the present. The present reveals the substance which lies within or behind all things and persons. . . .

Ossipon has by his unintentional complicity in Winnie's crime committed himself to that place out of place and time out of time where nothing exists but the eternal recurrence of the same. After he learns of Winnie's death he re-enacts in terrifying iteration, a repetition like Stevie's innumerable circles, Winnie's end as it was reported in the jargon of the newspaper. In the same way Winnie herself is haunted by the words which describe her anticipated death by hanging ('The drop given was fourteen feet'). Ossipon's brain 'pulsates wrongfully to the rhythm of journalistic phrases' (p. 311). He repeats to himself, or some anonymous power within him repeats for him, the banal words which are slowly driving him insane : 'An impenetrable mystery seems destined to hang for ever over this act of madness or despair.' (p. 307.) Death is not the obliteration of everything. It is that which cannot end. The denouement of *The Secret Agent* sets the impasse of the Professor against the disintegration of the robust Comrade Ossipon, his inability to 'think, work, sleep, . . . eat', and his absorption by the impersonal wakefulness which has claimed the other characters.

The last paragraphs of the novel juxtapose two walkers, Comrade Ossipon moving toward madness, despair, and the gutter, and the Professor, 'terrible in the simplicity of his idea calling madness and despair to the regeneration of the world'. This juxtaposition indicates that all the living deaths in the novel are the same death, and that the theme of *The Secret Agent* is the universal death which underlies life. As the characters get closer to death, they approach a condition in which they are equivalents of one another. There all 'I's' give way to a collective 'we', and communication is possible, communication not between persons, but within that which in each person is the same, the same secret agent at the heart of each.

The Professor can neither make a vacant place where spirit is able to build its own world, nor bring spirit into matter and transform the earth. The madness and despair which he calls on for the regeneration of the world are not pure emptiness of mind. They result from apprehension of the death which lies behind life. Death is a realm of madness because it is a place of contradiction, the copresence of motion and stillness, light and darkness, personality and anonymity, nothingness and substance, speech and silence, meaning and meaninglessness, servitude and freedom, time and eternity, beginning and ending held in a perpetual present. These pairs are all variations of one another, and, though the characters of *The Secret Agent* go toward death in different ways, most of them reach ultimately the same state, a state like that approached by the protagonists of Conrad's other novels, Kurtz, Marlow, Decoud, Flora de Barral, or Mrs Travers. Conrad's novels all say the same thing, and yet are all different, as all clouds differ and yet are children of the same sky. The Professor faces a double impossibility: the impossibility of escaping from the underlying substance of madness and despair, and the impossibility of using it in any way for the regeneration of the world. He can neither make a secure place where men can create their own culture, nor can he bring the darkness of madness and despair into the world as the foundation of a viable city of man. . . .

SOURCE: *Poets of Reality: Six Twentieth-Century Writers* (1965) pp. 39–67 – extracts.

NOTES

1. [Editor's Note.] These extracts are from the second section of chap ii of *Poets of Reality*. The section has been greatly cut – from over 11,000 words to 6,500; but the cuts are for the most part a matter of reducing the scale of illustration and quotation.

2. 'The Design of Conrad's *The Secret Agent*', *English Literary History*, XXII (1955) 148–64.

Norman Sherry

THE GREENWICH BOMB OUTRAGE AND *THE SECRET AGENT* (1967)

I

That the Greenwich Bomb Outrage of 1894 was the source for *The Secret Agent* has never been denied except by Conrad himself. In his earlier statements about the novel, Conrad emphasized that his story arose from that historic event. He wrote in the Author's Note to the novel:

the subject of *The Secret Agent* – I mean the tale – came to me in the shape of a few words uttered by a friend in a casual conversation about anarchists or rather anarchist activities. . . . Presently, passing to particular instances, we recalled the already old story of the attempt to blow up the Greenwich Observatory. . . . *This* book is *that* story, reduced to manageable proportions, its whole course suggested and centred round the absurd cruelty of the Greenwich Park explosion. (pp. ix–xii)[1]

And in a letter to Sir Algernon Methuen, 7 November 1906, he says: 'it is based on the inside knowledge of a certain event in the history of active anarchism'.[2] But in 1923, replying to Ambrose J. Barker, who had sent him a pamphlet on the subject, he denied all knowledge of the Greenwich Bomb Outrage which he had previously claimed as his source:

As a matter of fact I never knew anything of what was called . . . the 'Greenwich Bomb Outrage'. I was out of England when it happened, and thus I never read what was printed in the newspapers at the time. All I was aware of was the mere fact – my novel being, in intention, the history of Winnie Verloc.[3]

It looks very much as though Barker had stumbled upon one of Conrad's source books for the novel in this pamphlet and that Conrad's denial arose from a desire to conceal his sources of information. 'It was a matter of great interest to me', Conrad continued, presumably referring to the subject of the pamphlet, 'to see how near actuality I managed to come in a work of imagination.'

But Conrad's imagination required always a firm basis of fact, and he certainly had this basis of fact in the case of *The Secret Agent*. The novel derives undoubtedly from Conrad's knowledge of the Bomb Outrage and of anarchist activity in London at that time. In spite of his statement to the contrary, Conrad was, during January and February of 1894, living at 17 Gillingham Street, London, engaged in the writing of *Almayer's Folly*,[4] and must have read the accounts of the Greenwich Park incident which appeared in the London newspapers. Whatever part his imagination later gave to Winnie Verloc, his initial conception derived from the Bomb Outrage: the first draft of the novel was called *Verloc* after the protagonist, and Winnie's part in the first version to be published[5] is small.

His sources, as I shall show, were most certainly the contemporary newspaper accounts of, and speculation on, the incident. His 'inside knowledge' must have been in part derived from anarchist publications of the kind sold by Verloc, the secret agent, in his shop: 'a few apparently old copies of obscure newspapers, badly printed, with titles like *The Torch*, *The Gong* – rousing titles' (p. 3). And I believe that Conrad's source material can in part be traced to one anarchist newspaper, *The Anarchist*, and to two pamphlets on the Greenwich incident. One of these pamphlets – *The Greenwich Mystery* published in 1897 at Sheffield – may well be the one which Barker sent to Conrad and which until now has not been identified.[6] *The Anarchist* was at that time edited by a David Nicoll who was also author of the pamphlets.

The initial reports in the newspapers of the actual incident were as brief and as mysterious as that read out by Comrade Ossipon in the novel. *The Times* stated:

EXPLOSION IN GREENWICH PARK

Last evening an explosion was heard by a keeper of Greenwich Park on the hill close to the Royal Observatory. Proceeding thither he found a respectably-dressed man, in a kneeling posture, terribly mutilated.

One hand was blown off and the body was open. The injured man was only able to say, 'Take me home', and was unable to reply to a question as to where his home was. He was taken to the Seamen's Hospital on an ambulance, and died in less than half an hour.

A bottle, in many pieces, which had apparently contained an explosive substance, was found near the spot where the explosion took place, and it is conjectured that the deceased man fell and caused its contents to explode.

The deceased, who was not known in Greenwich, is a young man of about 30, supposed to be a foreigner. The only evidence of identification was a card bearing the name 'Bourbon' [sic]. (16 February 1894)

The *Morning Leader* reported the incident more sensationally, its headlines being:

BLOWN TO PIECES!

Victim an Anarchist (?)

Was he a member of a gang who had
fell designs on London's Safety?

A man who carried a terrible explosive blown to pieces at
Greenwich – it is declared that he was the chief of a gang of
anarchists, and was seeking to conceal his bombs – was he
an associate of Emile Henry?[7] (16 February 1894)

The victim's name was Martial Bourdin.

Although in *The Secret Agent* the reader has been prepared for an attempt to blow up the Greenwich Observatory by the interview between Verloc and Vladimir, the
explosion is introduced with as much shock and mystery
as was the actual explosion. Comrade Ossipon reads the
first newspaper report of Verloc's attempt to the Professor
– it is brief, and gives no explanations :

'Bomb in Greenwich Park. There isn't much so far. Half-
past eleven. Foggy morning. Effects of explosion felt as far
as Romney Road and Park Place. Enormous hole in the
ground under a tree filled with smashed roots and broken
branches. All round fragments of a man's body blown to
pieces. That's all. The rest's mere newspaper gup. No doubt
a wicked attempt to blow up the Observatory, they say.
H'm. That's hardly credible.' (pp. 70–1)

The two anarchists are unprepared for anything like this.
Ossipon knew of no such plan to blow up the Observatory, and the Professor knew only that there was 'to be a
demonstration against a building'. He had supplied Verloc with the explosive. They conclude that the shattered
body is that of Verloc. This misunderstanding is only
cleared up when Inspector Heat discovers, among the
remains of the body, the velvet collar of a coat bearing

a label on which is written Verloc's address. Through
this he eventually learns that the body is that of Stevie,
Verloc's witless brother-in-law.

It is obvious that the basic situations are the same
here. In both incidents there is an initial mystery as to
the identity of the victim, and much speculation as to
what happened to him in the Park and as to why he was
there. The major initial differences between the actual
and fictional incidents are in the fate of the victim and in
the cause of the accident.

Stevie is blown to pieces ('All round fragments of a
man's body blown to pieces'), and Conrad seems to have
taken the sensational headline of the *Morning Leader* –
'Blown to Pieces' – and for the purposes of his fiction
treated this as literal fact. Bourdin, on the other hand,
though badly wounded, was alive and able to speak when
he was discovered. The description of Bourdin's mutila-
tions was made much of in the *Morning Leader*:

His left hand and wrist were blown away, his face and the
rest of his body were covered with wounds, and his stomach
was blown open, a portion of the intestines protruding.
(16 February 1894)

In its report of the inquest, the paper gave such details
as:

On one of the iron bars of the fence, on the second bend
from the bottom, witness [a detective inspector] found a
tendon of sinew, fresh [*sic*], which had, by the force of the
impact, been twisted round the railing. Above that, and to
the left of the railing, he found five pieces of apparently
human skin. At a subsequent examination he found on the
right of the path two bones, apparently the knuckle-joints
of the thumb.

Conrad's descriptions of Stevie's death are not, therefore, out of place in the context of the general attitude to such gruesome details :

Another waterproof sheet was spread over that table in the manner of a tablecloth, with the corners turned up over a sort of mound – a heap of rags, scorched and bloodstained, half concealing what might have been an accumulation of raw material for a cannibal feast. (p. 86)

The listing of details which appears in the report of the inquest reflects the unmoved compilation of facts, however intolerable, by the police mind, and the attitude of Conrad's constable is the same :

'You used a shovel,' he remarked, observing a sprinkling of small gravel, tiny brown bits of bark, and particles of splintered wood as fine as needles.

'Had to in one place,' said the stolid constable. 'I sent a keeper to fetch a spade. When he heard me scraping the ground with it he leaned his forehead against a tree, and was as sick as a dog.' (p. 87)

'Well, here he is – all of him I could see. Fair. Slight – slight enough. Look at that foot there. I picked up the legs first, one after another. He was that scattered you didn't know where to begin.' (p. 89)

The effect in both newspaper and novel is macabre, but the newspaper reports also aroused sympathy in the reader for the condition and suffering of the mutilated man, Bourdin – conscious, after all, when found. This sympathy is denied Stevie by the fact that he is quite dead, and quite scattered. Heat's reflections that even instantaneous death might involve a moment of intense suffering cannot arouse our sympathies in face of the constable's descriptions and the image of Heat as 'an indigent customer bending over what may be called the by-products of a butcher's shop with a view to an inexpensive Sunday dinner' (p. 88).

Views on the cause of Bourdin's blowing himself up varied. The *Morning Leader* and *The Times* both suggested at first that Bourdin had stumbled, and that his death was, therefore, due to this accident :

He reached Greenwich about half an hour before dusk, and, turning to the left on leaving the station, he walked to the park by way of London-street and Stockwell-street. Walking along the main avenue lined with great trees on both sides, he reached the top of the hill, near the Observatory. Across the pathway the roots of the older trees protrude through the gravel, and it may be assumed that, it now being quite dusk, the man stumbled and fell, with the result that the infernal machine or machines which he was carrying exploded on his own person. (*The Times*, 16 February 1894)

But at the inquest on Bourdin, Colonel Majendie rejected this theory :

Beyond all doubt the man was standing up at the time of the explosion, which was not the result of an accidental fall on the part of either the deceased or the bomb. There was no disturbance on the gravel such as would have been found had any explosion occurred on the ground. (*Morning Leader*, 17 February 1894)

Colonel Majendie went so far as to reconstruct what occurred. He concluded that Bourdin had been holding the explosive in his left hand at a short distance in front of his body, while ascending the path; that he had taken the bottle of sulphuric acid out of his pocket, used as much of its contents as were necessary to ignite the bomb; and from some mischance, miscalculation, or clumsy handling the explosion, which was intended to occur very shortly, occurred prematurely.

In *The Secret Agent*, both the Professor and Verloc are convinced that Stevie had had plenty of time to deposit the bomb and leave the Park before it exploded: 'It was set for twenty minutes. . . . He either ran the time too close, or simply let the thing fall.' (p. 76.) But Conrad leaves us in no doubt as to why the bomb exploded, and he takes as the reason the view first put forward by the newspapers to explain Bourdin's accident – that he stumbled over the roots of trees in the dusk and fell. Conrad's constable, 'first man on the spot after the explosion', draws this same conclusion: 'Them roots do stick out all about the place. Stumbled against the root of a tree and fell, and that thing he was carrying must have gone off right under his chest.' (p. 89.)

Whereas Colonel Majendie gave elaborate evidence to prove that Bourdin could *not* have stumbled and fallen, Conrad goes to the trouble of giving equally convincing evidence that Stevie must have fallen. It was dusk when Bourdin died, and though Conrad's explosion takes place in the morning, it is a foggy morning to account for Stevie stumbling. Majendie pointed out that if Bourdin had stumbled his legs would have been wounded and there would have been disturbance to the ground beneath him. Stevie is blown to pieces, and there is a large hole where the explosion occurred.

The noise of the explosion is mentioned, as a piece of dramatic background material, in the *Morning Leader* report:

The stillness of the park . . . was rent by the sound of the explosion with such violence as to be heard by creditable

witnesses as far away as the Chatham and Dover Railway
Station in Stockwell-street on the west and Maze-hill station
on the South-Eastern Railway on the east. (16 February
1894)

This is paralleled by Conrad's : 'Effects of explosion felt
as far as Romney Road and Park Place.' (p. 70.)

Two schoolboys were first on the spot in the actual
case, followed by a park-keeper, Patrick Sullivan : 'He
declared that the report was followed by a volume of
smoke . . . and [he] immediately ran in the direction of
the smoke.' (*Morning Leader*, 20 February 1894.) A local
constable, one Patrick Tangey, was soon on the scene,
and he went afterwards to the Seamen's Hospital where
Bourdin had been taken. Constable Tangey searched the
body there, on the afternoon of the explosion, and a list
of the articles he found was given in the *Morning Leader*
(27 February 1894). In *The Secret Agent* it is the constable, of course, who arrives first, though he is provided
with a shovel by a park-keeper. Stevie is also carried to a
nearby hospital, and Chief Inspector Heat started 'immediately to begin his investigation on the spot [that is,
at Greenwich]. . . . Then he walked over to the hospital.'
He inspects the mangled remains and listens to the local
constable's report. Heat searches the body and takes away
an address.

Heat has been called from Scotland Yard to investigate the incident : '[He] had had a disagreeably busy
day since his department received the first *telegram*' (my
italics). In the same way, the newspapers report : 'The
local police officers quickly realised that they had more
than an ordinary case to deal with, and Scotland Yard
was communicated with by telegraph.' The report con-
tinues, 'One of the chiefs of the Criminal Investigation

Department proceeded at once to Greenwich' (*Morning Leader*, 16 February 1894).

These aspects of the investigation – the presence of the local constable, the taking of the remains to the hospital, the searching of the body, the sending for a Yard man by telegraph, are I believe too close to the original for Conrad not to have been working with that original in mind.

At the inquest on Bourdin, two witnesses gave evidence of his journey by tram to the Park :

The tram conductor who issued the ticket, William Smith, stated that last Thursday week he was working on the Westminster to East Greenwich Route. He only issued one through ticket. . . . He issued it to a young man whom he believed to be the deceased. The man sat about half-way down on the left hand side when he got in first. As the people gradually got out he moved up to the front end of the car, nearer to the driver. He did not appear to be carrying anything in particular. He travelled right down to the terminus at East Greenwich. (*Morning Leader*, 27 February 1894)

John Bone, a timekeeper, stated that while he was checking the conductor's time, the deceased asked the conductor the way to Greenwich Park.

Stevie, on the other hand, travelled by train, but evidence of the journey is also given by two witnesses :

The porter who took the tickets at Maze Hill remembers two chaps answering to the description passing the barrier. They seemed to him two respectable working-men of a superior sort – sign painters or house-decorators. The big man got out of a third-class compartment backward, with a bright tin can in his hand. On the platform he gave it to carry to the fair young fellow who followed him. (p. 107)

The old woman who spoke to the sergeant noticed a fair-haired fellow coming out of Maze Hill Station. . . . She noticed two men coming out of the station after the up-train had gone on. . . . She couldn't tell if they were together. She took no particular notice of the big one, but the other was a fair, slight chap, carrying a tin varnish can in one hand. . . . (p. 88)

The nature of the evidence and the way in which it is presented by Conrad is similar to that of the actual case.

Many reasons were given at the time to account for Bourdin's presence with the explosive in Greenwich Park. Certainly, he was connected in the newspaper reports with the anarchists from the beginning. In its first report of the incident, the *Morning Leader* quoted the Central News Agency's account of the events before Bourdin blew himself to pieces:

But these facts among others are beyond dispute, that the inquiries of the detectives, although cautiously made, frightened the [anarchist] plotters, that the gang hurriedly scattered, and that its chief met with a horrible death last evening when endeavouring in a panic of fear to carry away to some place the deadly explosives. . . . (16 February 1894)

On 19 February, the newspaper put forward a different theory, one which accounted for the fact that Bourdin had travelled unnecessarily far – from Tottenham Court Road to Greenwich – with his infernal machine:

Beyond all question, Bourdin was well aware of the fact that he was being watched . . . and the theory has been set up that, instead of taking the train straight to Dover, he, with a view to eluding the observations of the detectives and of a police spy who was supposed to be on his track, got out at New-cross, his intention being to baffle his pursuers and catch a later train for the South Coast. It is thought that while thus waiting, he, in order to kill time, went for a ramble in the neighbourhood and found himself in Greenwich-park, where he was so soon destined to meet his terrible fate.

This was a pretty tall story and was not repeated by the newspaper. Anarchist friends of Bourdin held a different view :

Their idea is that he went to the park with a new combination of explosives of his own invention with the intention of trying how it would work. They believe that he intended going to some remote part of the park and there making the experiment. They do not for a moment conceive that he had any design against the Royal Observatory, as he had, they say quaintly, 'no spite against that building'. (*Morning Leader*, 17 February 1894)

Another view put forward was that Bourdin had a rendezvous at Greenwich Park with other anarchists in order to hand over chemicals to them. Yet another was that the anarchists had to move the explosives away from one hiding place which might be raided to an out-of-the-way park like Greenwich :

a comparatively unfrequented park like that of Greenwich, which abounds in solitary spots, where a man might even dig with a reasonable prospect of not being observed, offered a desirable resort. But against this theory, it is pointed out, may be placed the fact that there are parks which are much easier of access – to say nothing of the river – to a man living off the Tottenham-court Rd. than Greenwich could have been. (*Morning Leader*, 17 February 1894)

Then it was declared that 'possession of explosives had become very risky and [he] resolved to get rid of his share of the "stuff" by using it against some Government building' (*Morning Leader,* 17 February 1894).

Conrad adopted the explanation which had the support of the Government, that Bourdin was in fact out to destroy the Greenwich Observatory. *The Times,* 17 February 1894, argues very forcibly for the view that Martial Bourdin was going to demonstrate against the Observatory :

Whether his actual intention was to blow up the Observatory at Greenwich or not is one of those questions which can be judged from probabilities only, since the person who could have spoken with certainty upon the point is dead, but the facts certainly show that he intended some serious mischief when he entered Greenwich Park; and the path which he followed, a narrow, zigzag, and secluded path, leads practically nowhere except to the Observatory.

Moreover, at the inquest on Bourdin, Colonel Majendie, when asked by the coroner what he thought was the man's intention, answered :

Probably against the Observatory, or its contents, or its inmates. That is my opinion. I can arrive at no other conclusion. (*Morning Leader,* 27 February 1894)

One of Conrad's major changes from source to novel would appear to be that Stevie was accompanied by his brother-in-law, Mr Verloc, to Greenwich Park whereas Bourdin made the journey to Greenwich alone. However, as the investigation into Bourdin's movements before he blew himself up got under way, new information appeared. It was discovered that 'he lunched at about two o'clock with his brother . . . at the International Restaurant, Bennet St., Fitzroy Square. . . . It was ten minutes to three when he left.' (*Morning Leader,* 17 February

1894.) Two days later, an interview with Samuels, Bourdin's brother-in-law, was published in the *Morning Leader* :

MR SAMUELS INTERVIEWED

What Bourdin's brother-in-law has to say of his Purpose.

Mr H. B. Samuels, the editor of one of the Anarchist papers, has, of course, been interviewed. He is, besides being an Anarchist leader, a brother-in-law of Bourdin. He stated that on Thursday last he met Bourdin in the West-end about two o'clock, and remained in his company a considerable time. During the conversation he asked Bourdin whether he had succeeded in finding work. The latter replied in the negative, and added that he did not particularly want any at that time. Mr Samuels told him that probably if he accompanied him to the place he worked at he would be able to get some work, as they were very busy. . . . They walked about 20 or 30 yards together in the direction of Mr Samuels' workshop, when Bourdin suddenly exclaimed, 'No, I'm not going to-day. I shall go back.' They then parted. Mr Samuels thinks it very unlikely that he had anything of an explosive nature on his person at that time. He thinks Bourdin must have had an appointment to meet someone soon afterwards, from whom he obtained the explosive. By the way, Mr Samuels subsequently said he had an idea that the manufacture of bombs for Continental use has been going on for some little time. He feels convinced Bourdin did not go to Greenwich with any intention of blowing up the Observatory. His object was, he believes, either to buy the explosive or to experiment.

The Anarchist leader was greatly surprised to learn that a sum of £13 in gold had been found in his brother-in-law's possession, and it was a complete mystery to him as to where he obtained the money. He was quite certain, he said, that when Bourdin left him he had scarcely any money on him, and only the previous night at the restaurant where it was their custom to have supper he left without paying and the same thing had occurred the day before that. Mr Samuels declared that Bourdin was quite unacquainted with the neighbourhood of Greenwich, and therefore he considered it probable that whoever gave him the explosives also gave him definite instructions as to where to go and what to do.

We have here the fundamental situation involving Verloc and his brother-in-law. Samuels was married to Bourdin's sister, Bourdin was the victim of the explosion in Greenwich Park – an explosion surrounded by mystery – and Samuels was in the company of Bourdin not long before the explosion took place. Moreover, Samuels, like Verloc, was a leading anarchist. Thus the pattern of events and personages immediately surrounding the disaster was completed in substantially the form in which Conrad was to present it in his novel.

Up to this point, we can conclude that Conrad was making the kind of use of the actual incident that one would expect of this author who worked close to facts and obviously knew the facts in some detail in this instance. Certainly the initial impact of the Greenwich mystery, the nature of the incident, and even the 'flavour' imparted to the inquiry through newspaper reports, is there in *The Secret Agent*.

II

The Greenwich mystery remained the Greenwich 'mystery' to the public. No real background information as to Bourdin's anarchist activities appeared. And the speculation in the newspapers is a reflection of the mysteriousness of the event. Thus the quality of the initial incident which attracted Conrad was its inexplicableness, as he records in his Author's Note :

> a blood-stained inanity of so fatuous a kind that it was impossible to fathom its origin by any reasonable or even unreasonable process of thought. For perverse unreason has its own logical processes. But that outrage could not be laid hold of mentally in any sort of way, so that one remained faced by the fact of a man blown to bits for nothing even most remotely resembling an idea, anarchistic or other. (p. x)

Conrad enhanced the inanity of the event by making the victim the half-witted and unallied Stevie. At the same time he removed the mysterious element by evolving a chain of events which led perversely but logically to Stevie's death. Vladimir tells Verloc that he must organize some anarchist activity of a kind which will centre public interest on the movement. He suggests blowing up the Greenwich Observatory. Behind this suggestion is the desire of European powers that the British should be shocked by an example of anarchy in their own country and so be persuaded to stop offering sanctuary to anarchists from the Continent and introduce repressive legislation against them. The Bomb Outrage is, therefore, the result of a desire to bring the anarchist movement into disrepute in England.

No suggestion of intrigue of this kind appeared in the newspapers of the time, but Conrad could have found it, set out with much indignation, in the anarchist press, and particularly in David Nicoll's pamphlet *The Greenwich Mystery*.

Nicoll's purpose in writing his pamphlet was not merely to elucidate the Greenwich mystery, but to unmask Samuels as a police agent. In a later pamphlet, *Letters from the Dead*, in which he continued his task of unmasking, he wrote : 'I am glad my task is over. I did not seek it. It was forced upon me by those who allowed a scoundrel to escape without exposure.' (p. 8.)

The Greenwich mystery thus becomes a police plot to bring the anarchists into disrepute in England, a plot which made use of a double agent and in the carrying out of which the tool used by this double agent was accidentally killed. In neither the fictional nor the actual circumstances was the plot notably successful in its aims. In the actual case there was a mob demonstration against the anarchists,[8] a question in the House of Commons, and certain murmurings in the press, but generally the affair was played down. Mr Asquith, in answer to Colonel Howard Vincent's question as to whether 'in the circumstances of the day, the Government proposed to place any limit upon foreign immigration', said :

Her Majesty's Government are not of opinion that, in this respect, any necessity has arisen for a change in the law which has so long prevailed in Great Britain, and which they believe to be sufficient both for our own protection and for the due performance of our international duties. (*The Times*, 20 February 1894)

And Conrad in *The Secret Agent* plays it down by means of his Assistant Commissioner : 'it is not the work of anarchism at all, but of something else altogether – some species of authorized scoundrelism. . . . I call it an episode, because this affair . . . is episodic; it is no part of any general scheme, however wild.' (pp. 140–1.)

Fundamentally, therefore, Conrad's anarchist plot, which is actually a political plot, was based in nearly all its aspects upon the truth behind the Greenwich Outrage – the truth, we should note, as it was put forward by the anarchist press. Even the fear and indignation over the plot expressed by Ossipon is based upon the actual re-action of the anarchists in England at that time.

Verloc is too indolent to cut much of a figure as an active anarchist. And yet he is more than a mere anarch-ist. Despite his indolence, he acts, however ineffectually, as a double agent – he supplies information not only to the Embassy, but also to the British police. Urged by Vladimir, he becomes an *agent provocateur*. Conrad did not find a prototype for Verloc's character in Samuels, but he did find a prototype of the double agent and the *agent provocateur*. The sinister double agent behind the death of Bourdin was his brother-in-law, Samuels.

So far as Nicoll was concerned, the Greenwich mystery had *not* been solved by the time he wrote his pamphlet of 1897, three years after the event: 'the Greenwich Mystery is still a mystery', he stated, and he asked : 'What was the object of Bourdin in going to Greenwich Park?' The solution of the Greenwich mystery, for Nicoll, and the reason for Bourdin being in the Park lay with Samuels. According to Nicoll, Samuels sent Bourdin off with the explosive, intending that he should be arrested by the police with the explosive on him – a more ruthless action than that of Mr Verloc, who intended only that Stevie should act as a carrier. Conrad stresses that Verloc 'never meant Stevie to perish with such abrupt violence' (p. 187) and we must assume, in spite of the radical differences that appear between the apathetic Verloc and the aggres-sive Samuels, that Samuels did not anticipate that *his* brother-in-law would 'perish with such abrupt violence'.

Nicoll's evidence against Samuels begins with Samuels's statements as to his meeting with Bourdin immediately before the explosion :

Mr Samuels told the 'Central News', he was in Bourdin's

company at two o'clock, and remained in his company for *a considerable time*. How long is a considerable time? Forty minutes! If so, Bourdin must have left him to start on his journey to Greenwich. As it is known Bourdin travelled by tram, it would have taken him from 2.40 to 4.20 p.m., one hour and forty minutes to reach Greenwich from Hanover Square. We have tested this by actual experiment. He was in Samuels' company at 2 p.m., and arrived at Greenwich at 4.20 according to the evidence of the tram conductor. (p. 6)

Nicoll draws the conclusion that Samuels must have been in Bourdin's company 'a considerable time after 2 p.m.'. If this was the case it makes nonsense of Samuels's own story that he walked only '20 or 30 yards' with Bourdin before Bourdin left him and casts doubt on his further suggestion that 'Bourdin must have had an appointment to meet someone soon afterwards, from whom he obtained the explosive' and that 'whoever gave him [Bourdin] the explosives also gave him definite instructions as to where to go and what to do'. Nicoll also quotes a Press Association report:

In the course of the same afternoon he [Bourdin] was observed in company with another man, in the neighbourhood of Hanover Square, and later on the two parted company in Whitehall, Bourdin then walking over Westminster Bridge and taking the tram to Greenwich. (p. 5)

Inevitably he asks the question: 'Did the mysterious stranger in Hanover Square, and Whitehall, bear any resemblance to Mr Samuels? How did he escape arrest?' (p. 6).

It is Nicoll's belief that Samuels gave the explosive to Bourdin:

My opinion is, that he was asked by Samuels to take the money and the 'brown paper parcel' to some mysterious 'comrade' whom he was to meet in that neighbourhood. He was too weak to refuse; but showed some reluctance, so the tempter was forced to go with him part of the way 'to give him courage'. (p. 15)

And at a later date, it seems, Samuels admitted that he supplied Bourdin with explosive and that he had accompanied him for a considerable distance on his journey. Nicoll records that, at a weekly meeting of the 'Commonweal group', Samuels made the following statement:

As to the Bourdin affair, he declared he had stolen the explosives out of the house of a comrade D . . . who had them for use in his business, and given them to Bourdin. Further, he admitted that he went with Bourdin on his way to Greenwich, nearly as far as Westminster Bridge. That they were pursued by detectives, and parted there. One to go to his death, while the other returned peacefully home, unmolested by the police. (*The Greenwich Mystery*, p. 13)

Apparently, Samuels had been giving explosives to his fellow anarchists, and then informing on them, so that they could be arrested by the police for being in possession of explosives. Nicoll quotes an incident to prove this:

But that night, in the street, he [R . . .] met an acquaintance who was evidently in a high state of excitement. 'Have you heard the news,' he exclaimed, 'Samuels has been giving explosives to J . . . *and two days after J . . .'s house was raided by the police*. They evidently expected to find something, for *they tore up the boards of the floor*.' (p. 12)

Samuels was not simply intending to betray his fellow anarchists by these methods. The implications of his actions went much further as Mrs Bevington, a well-known anarchist, pointed out in a letter to Nicoll after the appearance of and in reply to his pamphlet. She accepts Samuels's guilt, considers him to be a traitor, and also to be in league with the police in order to bring the anarchist movement into disrepute:

Dear Comrade, – You have got the Bourdin history wrong. The facts were that Samuels having, as it is said on good authority, supplied him with the *new compound*, suggested to him to take it somewhere for the purpose of *experiment*. Well, Bourdin, in all good faith, thought 'experiment' *meant* experiment; and hit on Epping Forest as a place where he would have a good chance of exploding his compound against a big tree without great danger of its being heard, or him seen before he could get away. *This would, however, have obviously been of little use to the police; quite obviously a mere experiment – or else a mere bit of foolish mischief for a big lucrative scare and scandal.* [My italics.] Well, as the fates had it, Samuels met him just as he was starting with his ingredients. 'I'm going,' says Bourdin, touching his pockets significantly. 'Where to?' 'Epping Forest.' 'Oh, don't go there, go to Greenwich Park.' 'All right,' and they went together as far as Westminster, and were seen; and one of them accordingly was made the butt of the police. How do I know Samuels told him where to go? Because Mrs Samuels, [this is Bourdin's sister] whom I used to see very often at that time, *told me*. Why do I report that conversation above? Because Samuels himself, before he was suspected by the Group, and while he was still desirous of seeming an important character in the eyes of sundry gaping comrades, boastingly related it. (*Letters from the Dead*, p. 3)[9]

Mrs Bevington's account of the mystery is therefore that Samuels gave Bourdin a compound to experiment with but in order that the experiment should produce 'a big lucrative scare and scandal', for the purpose of bringing disgrace upon the anarchist movement, he deliberately directed Bourdin to Greenwich Park. Thus the mere fact of Bourdin being discovered near the Observatory in possession of an explosive would be taken to be an attempt upon the Observatory. This is the basis of Conrad's plot. Vladimir's decision that Verloc should bomb the Observatory stems directly from Samuels's attempt to discredit the anarchists in England.

Nicoll quotes Samuels's suggestion (which appeared in the *Sheffield Daily Telegraph*, 15 February 1894) that the Bourdin incident was '*the commencement of an extensive plot*' and this suggestion, Nicoll argues, 'spread terror among the timid middle class and Conservative Newspapers raised at once an outcry'. He quotes from *The Globe* leader: 'Society is asking how long the British metropolis will be content to afford a safe asylum for gangs of assassins, who there plot and perfect atrocious schemes for universal murder on the Continent.' And Nicoll comments that 'The enemies of the right of asylum saw at once that the Greenwich explosion, and the statements of Mr Samuels were a great help to them in their agitation'. Thus, the agitation which gathered as a result of the Greenwich Outrage, and which is commented upon here, is made the source of Vladimir's speculation as to how the middle classes can be stirred in England. As Mrs Bevington says: 'a big lucrative scare and scandal' indeed!

An example of the kind of reaction that was hoped for from the Greenwich Park explosion appears in chap. 10 of *The Secret Agent* when the Lady Patroness, after having spoken to Vladimir, turns to the Assistant Commissioner and says:

He [Vladimir] has been threatening society with all sorts

of horrors . . . apropos of this explosion in Greenwich Park.
It appears we all ought to quake in our shoes at what's com-
ing if those people are not suppressed all over the world.
I had no idea this was such a grave affair. (pp. 223–4)

And Conrad may have derived the idea of Vladimir
and the foreign embassy providing the initial impetus
for the Bomb Outrage from the following passages taken
from *The Anarchist,* which was edited by the author of
The Greenwich Mystery, David Nicoll :

The Russian and other Continental despotisms are very
anxious to lay hands on the refugees from their tyranny,
men whose names are known throughout the civilised world
for their courage and high character.
    A few dynamite explosions in England would suit the
book of the Russian police splendidly, and might even
result in terrifying the English bourgeoisie into handing
over the refugees to the vengeance of the Russian Czar.
(*The Anarchist,* March 1894)

the victims of one of the numerous foreign police spies
with which London abounds. The Russian Government
alone are said to have some thirty of these busy gentlemen
in their pay, and they must do something to earn their
money.
    England is now almost the only country where the rebels
against the tyranny of the despots of the Continent can
find refuge, and the despots would like very much to see
the right of asylum swept away. 'Plots to blow up the Royal
Exchange' are very useful for this purpose. . . . (*The Anarchist,* 13 May 1894)

The reaction of the anarchist Ossipon in the novel to
the explosion is one of fear and is based fairly accurately
on the reaction of contemporary anarchists to the Greenwich Explosion :

'No doubt a wicked attempt to blow up the Observatory, they say. H'm. That's hardly credible. . . . I hadn't the slightest idea – not the ghost of a notion of anything of the sort being planned to come off here – in this country. Under the present circumstances it's nothing short of criminal . . . this business may affect our position very adversely in this country. . . . I assure you that we in London had no knowledge.' (pp. 71–4)

The *Morning Leader* on 19 February 1894 carried the opinions of certain anarchists :

there has been a seemingly very frank confession on their part that the occurrence took them completely by surprise.

A young German anarchist put it as follows :

comrades from the Continent – whatever might be their intentions abroad – had found a safe shelter in London, and it was hardly likely, he added, that they would commit themselves to a line of desperate action in this country, which could only result in their losing the protection and immunity from arrest which they now enjoyed. . . . Anarchists were not so blind to their own interests and well-being as to forgo by their conduct the right to the asylum which England so generousiy offered to political refugees. . . . As to Bourdin's plan, he personally had not the slightest knowledge, but he did not for one moment think that the deceased ever intended to make an attempt to blow up the Observatory.

Conrad records in his Author's Note his gratification that 'a visitor from America informed him that all sorts of revolutionary refugees in New York would have it that **the book** was written by somebody who knew a lot about them' (p. xiv). A comparison of the newspapers and anarchist publications of the time with the novel makes

this statement a less surprising one since it is apparent
that Conrad obtained from his sources not only the motives and attitudes of anarchists of that time but a whole
series of related events based upon the secret workings of
police and anarchists in London which led to the Greenwich Outrage. Moreover, an 'anarchy' of a different kind
— the 'inanity' and 'perverse unreason' exhibited by the
ironic universe of *The Secret Agent* — was already to hand
for Conrad in the actual event.

But Conrad's insistence upon Winnie Verloc as the
central figure of the story derives from her importance
in the imaginative process which turned a public event
into a domestic drama. The only reference to the reaction
of Samuels's wife to the death of her brother that I have
been able to find is in the letter by Mrs Bevington. It suggests a reaction on Mrs Samuels's part which is only un-
derstandable if she is understood to be a woman under
the complete dominance of her husband. Mrs Bevington
describes how, after the death of Bourdin, when Samuels
had visited her and proceeded to give instruction for
making and charging bombs, she 'asked Mrs Samuels
what she thought of all this ! ! "Oh, it is all right", she
said; "I should have objected only a little while ago;
but not now I understand the question better." ' Had
this been Winnie Verloc's reaction, *The Secret Agent*
would have been contained within the bounds of the
anarchist world, with all that it implied, at least in Conrad's view, of actions and ideas unrelated to anything
but their own futility. But, while he was thinking of the
novel, 'Slowly the dawning of Mrs Verloc's maternal
passion grew up to a flame'[10] and the novel was no longer
concerned solely with the anarchist plot. It is Winnie
Verloc's 'secret ardour' which enables her to accept her
life as Verloc's wife, to ignore his short-comings and his
mysterious occupation, and which ultimately forces her

to murder Verloc. Obviously to Conrad Winnie Verloc's reaction is the 'true' reaction to the tragedy as Mrs Samuels's reaction was not. For this reason Conrad could write 'Personally I have never had any doubt of the reality of Mrs Verloc's story'[11] even though that part of his novel was not, so far as I have been able to discover, based on fact.

SOURCE: *Review of English Studies*, n.s., XVIII (1967) 412–28.

NOTES

For a fuller study, see Norman Sherry, *Conrad's Western World* (Cambridge : Cambridge University Press, 1971).

1. Page references to *The Secret Agent* are to the *Collected Edition of the Works of Joseph Conrad* (London, 1947).

2. G. Jean-Aubry, *Joseph Conrad: Life and Letters* (London, 1927) II 38.

3. Ibid., p. 322.

4. Jocelyn Baines, *Joseph Conrad* (London, 1959) p. 133, and Eloise Knapp Hay, *The Political Novels of Joseph Conrad* (Chicago, 1963) p. 228.

5. A serial version of the novel appeared in *Ridgway's Militant Weekly*, from 6 October to 15 December 1906.

6. According to Jean-Aubry, the pamphlet was about the attempt to blow up the Greenwich Observatory and it quoted *The Times*'s description of the perpetrator of the crime (Jean-Aubry, *Life and Letters*, II 322, n. 2).

7. Emile Henry was a French anarchist who, three days before the explosion at Greenwich, had thrown a bomb into a restaurant which killed one person and injured twenty others. Conrad probably had this incident in mind

when he has Vladimir lecture Verloc on the uselessness of such attacks : 'A murderous attempt on a restaurant . . . would suffer . . . from the suggestion of a non-political passion.' (p. 32.)

8. 'The funeral of the Anarchist Bourdin . . . took place on Friday, Feb. 23, in Finchley Cemetery . . . an Anarchist who attempted to deliver a speech at the grave was promptly suppressed by the police, who had afterwards to protect him from the violence of the crowd. The windows of the Autonomie Club [well-known Anarchist meeting-place] were broken, and a mob in Fitzroy Square indulged in anti-Anarchist manifestations.' (*The Illustrated London News*, 3 Mar 1894.)

9. A second pamphlet on the Greenwich mystery made up of letters by Nicoll and others (London, 1898).

10. Author's Note to *The Secret Agent*, p. xii.

11. Ibid., p. xiii.

Ian Watt

THE POLITICAL AND SOCIAL BACKGROUND OF *THE SECRET AGENT*

Norman Sherry (pp. 202–28 above) presents a meticulous account of the main historical source of *The Secret Agent*, the Greenwich Park explosion of 14 February 1894. The modern reader, however, may find it useful to have some further information about the wider background of the affair, and about Conrad's other sources.

This is not to imply that *The Secret Agent* is to be considered a novel about an actual historical event, in the sense that Josephine Tey's *The Franchise Affair*, say, is a fictional reconstruction of the mysterious Elizabeth Canning case in which Henry Fielding participated. For although Joseph Conrad's fiction nearly always started from some germ of reality – an anecdote, an historical event, an incident seen or a conversation overheard – by the time the work was finished it usually disclaimed any relation to actual persons, places or events. The germ of *Lord Jim*, for example, the desertion of the pilgrim ship, was a widely reported and notorious event; but in the completed novel Conrad tried to remove any details that tied it down to an identifiable place and time.

In *The Secret Agent* Conrad was hardly free to avoid specifying London and Greenwich as his locale; and he retained a good many of the actual details of the event. On the other hand, as the Author's Note says, after the initial challenge of his 'friend's' offhand remarks about

the explosion, Conrad proceeded to develop the germinal
cluster of ideas with the utmost imaginative freedom.

Conrad also steadfastly denied, and I think rather more
legitimately than Sherry seems to allow (p. 202 above),
any detailed knowledge either of the explosion itself or
of anarchism in general. As regards anarchism, Conrad's letter of 7 October 1907 to R. B. Cunninghame
Graham is particularly explicit :

. . . I am glad you like the *S. Agent*. *Vous comprenez bien*
that the story was written completely without malice. It
had some importance for me as a new departure in *genre*
and as a sustained effort in ironical treatment of a melodramatic subject, – which was my technical intention. . . .

Every word you say I treasure. It's no use, I cannot conceal my pride in your praise. It is an immense thing for
me, however great the part I ascribe to the generosity of
your mind and the warmth of your heart.

But I don't think that I've been satirizing the revolutionary world. All these people are not revolutionaries, –
they are shams. And as regards the Professor, I did not
intend to make him despicable. He is incorruptible at any
rate. In making him say : 'Madness and despair, – give me
that for a lever and I will move the world', I wanted to give
him a note of perfect sincerity. At the worst he is a mega-
lomaniac of an extreme type. And every extremist is respectable.

I am extremely flattered to have secured your commenda-
tion for my Secretary of State and for the Revolutionary
Toodles. It was very easy there (for me) to go utterly wrong.

By Jove ! If I had the necessary talent I would like to go
for the true anarchist, which is the millionaire. Then you
would see the venom flow. But it's too big a job. . . .[1]

Conrad's emphasis here that anarchism in *The Secret
Agent* is treated 'without malice' no doubt arises from
his anxiety not to offend Cunninghame Graham's radical

views. Yet there is much other evidence to show that Conrad did not think of *The Secret Agent* either as a serious study of anarchism, or even as a responsible reconstruction of the explosion itself. It is true that Conrad stated to Methuen that the story was 'based on the inside knowledge of a certain event in the history of active anarchism' : but he also went on to insist that 'otherwise it is *purely a work of imagination*'. Nearly twenty years later Conrad repeated this qualification in a letter to Ambrose J. Barker, who had sent him a pamphlet about the Greenwich Outrage, presumably that by David Nicoll mentioned above. On 1 September 1923 Conrad replied :

Thank you very much for your letter and the pamphlet in which I was very much interested.

As a matter of fact I never knew anything of what was called, if I remember rightly, the 'Greenwich Bomb Outrage'. I was out of England when it happened, and thus I never read what was printed in the newspapers at the time. All I was aware of was the mere fact – my novel being, in intention, the history of Winnie Verloc. I hope you have seen that the purpose of the book was not to attack any doctrine, or even the men holding that doctrine. My object, apart from the aim of telling a story, was to hold up the worthlessness of certain individuals and the baseness of some others. It was a matter of great interest to me to see how near actuality I managed to come in a work of imagination.

I hope you will do me the pleasure to accept the book [*The Rover*] I am sending you – which is also a work of pure imagination though very different in subject and treatment from the *Secret Agent*.

P.S. I suppose you meant me to keep the pamphlet, which I would like to paste into my own copy of the novel.[2]

But if we must agree that *The Secret Agent* is not a novel about a particular event, and that its merits, therefore, do not depend upon the accuracy or insight with which the event is reconstructed, the opposite extreme also seems to me equally untenable. If *The Secret Agent* dealt with events, characters and ideas that had no basis whatever in the real world or human history, we should presumably have to read it as fantasy; but the novel surely enlists a quite different kind of credence, and makes more serious claims on our attention. More information about the background of *The Secret Agent* may help, then, not to test the authenticity of its interpretation of historical events, but to suggest what distance exists between Conrad's fictional world, and the actual time and *milieu* with which his novel deals.

It is impossible to establish with any precision how far Conrad's version departs from the facts about the Greenwich Observatory explosion, because these facts are still not fully known. This is really quite in the normal course of things for a not particularly important event in which the protagonist died, and in which secret police, double agents, and possibly foreign powers, were involved. Nevertheless, enough is known to make it possible to show that on some issues Conrad was close to the facts, and that on others he departed from them. There is, of course, a third category of matters on which there is insufficient evidence to make a judgement.

Sherry shows that Conrad's version was faithful in its general outlines to what the newspapers reported about the explosion in Greenwich Park, and how the anarchists reacted to it.

There is also some evidence to show that the Criminal Investigation Department was directly involved in the affair through a secret agent pretending to be an anarchist, who possibly inspired the Greenwich Outrage, and who almost certainly provided the explosives. Here the evidence comes from three main sources: from David Nicoll, whose two pamphlets on the matter are quoted above; from Ford Madox Ford; and from Sir Robert Anderson's memoirs.

Nicoll himself believed that Bourdin's brother-in-law, the former editor of an anarchist journal, *Commonweal*, H. B. Samuels, was a police spy who had sent Bourdin to his fate; and Samuels's loyalty to the movement was certainly questioned at the time by other anarchists. That the police had some informant about Bourdin's plans is obliquely confirmed by Sir Robert Anderson in a later memoir than the one Conrad quoted in his Author's Note. Anderson writes:

I never spent hours of greater anxiety than during one afternoon in February, 1894, when information reached me that a French tailor named Bourdin had left his shop in Soho with a bomb in his pocket. To track him was impracticable. All that could be done was to send out officers in every direction to watch persons and places that he might be likely to attack. His actual objective was the very last place the Police would have thought of watching, namely Greenwich Observatory. Travelling to Greenwich by tramcar, he entered the Park, and as he ascended the path leading to the Observatory he evidently took the bomb out of his pocket, and was preparing to use it, when it exploded in his hand, inflicting injuries from which he died after a few hours suffering.[3]

Anderson gives no further details – he is using Bourdin only as an illustration of how difficult it is 'to catch a criminal who works alone' and especially 'these fiends . . . the alien anarchist dynamiters'. If Samuels was in fact the informer, it sounds as though Samuels left

Bourdin without knowing where he was going, so that he could not warn the police in time.

Nicoll mentions another police informer, Auguste Coulon, who started an anarchist journal on behalf of the police, and who was also watching Bourdin; but Anderson does not help establish what went wrong with the surveillance, and this aspect of the case remains a mystery. On other matters, however, Anderson is more helpful. In particular he confirms Conrad's picture of the conflict between a newly appointed Assistant Commissioner of Scotland Yard and such 'old departmental hands' as Conrad's Chief Inspector Heat. When Anderson moved from the political Secret Service to the Criminal Investigation Department he was, he tells us,

not a little surprised . . . to find occasion to suspect that one of my principal subordinates was trying to impose on me as though I were an ignoramus. For when any important crime of a certain kind occurred, and I set myself to investigate *à la* Sherlock Holmes, he used to listen to me in the way that so many people listen to sermons in church; and when I was done he would stolidly announce that the crime was the work of A, B, C, or D, naming some of his stock heroes. Though a keen and shrewd police officer, the man was unimaginative, and I thus accounted for the fact that his list was always brief, and that the same names came up repeatedly. It was 'Old Carr', or 'Wirth', or 'Sausage', or 'Shrimps', or 'Quiet Joe', or 'Red Bob', &c. &c. one name or another being put forward according to the kind of crime I was investigating.[4]

It was actually only by an accident arising out of such conflicts within the police authority that the use of double agents by the Secret Service had come to public attention in the years previous to 1894. The matter is very fully set forth in the book of Anderson's which Conrad quotes in his Author's Note, *Sidelights on the Home Rule Movement*. Anderson had been in secret correspondence for over twenty years with one Major Henri Le Caron, the pseudonym of Thomas M. Beach, an Englishman who had risen high in the American Fenian movement, the Clan-na-Gael. Caron had given Anderson a great deal of important advance information about the bombing and other plans of the Fenians. Inevitably, in Anderson's view, Caron had acted as an *agent provocateur* in some of these cases.[5] The nature of Caron's activities became public during the Parnell case. In an interview with Parnell, Caron had learned of Parnell's general awareness of the plans for violence of the Irish Land League. This and other information about the relationships between the parliamentary and the revolutionary wings of the fight for Irish independence was eventually used, and falsified, in the 1887 *Times* articles on 'Parnellism and Crime'. In the Special Commission of investigation that followed, Caron appeared as a witness; and his testimony revealed both the extent to which the Government used double agents and *agents provocateurs*, and the way that they and their immediate superiors could influence public policy. As a result the secret use of Caron's evidence to support Conservative policy on Ireland was attacked by the Liberal leader Sir William Harcourt, who rightly believed that the alleged *Times* letter from Parnell to the dynamitard Patrick Egan was a forgery. Harcourt was also concerned at the way Anderson had employed Caron without even informing the then Home Secretary, Henry Matthews; and Anderson then defended the need to keep Caron's activities entirely to himself in a letter to *The Times*.[6]

In view of his letter to Barker it is perhaps wiser to differ from Sherry, and assume that Conrad had not read

Nicoll's pamphlets, and that his main informant for the
background of *The Secret Agent* was Ford Madox Ford,
the 'friend' mentioned in Conrad's Author's Note. In his
memoir of Conrad written immediately after Conrad's
death, Ford contradicts part of Conrad's version of their
colloquy :

What the writer really did say to Conrad was : 'Oh that
fellow was half an idiot : His sister murdered her husband
afterwards and was allowed to escape by the police. I remember the funeral.' . . . The suicide was invented by Conrad. And the writer knew – and Conrad knew that the
writer knew – a great many anarchists of the Goodge Street
group, as well as a great many of the police who watched
them. The writer had provided Conrad with Anarchist
literature, with memoirs, with introductions to at least one
Anarchist young lady who figures in *The Secret Agent*.[7]

There is no other evidence that Bourdin was 'half an
idiot' or that his sister murdered her husband; and in any
case Ford's testimony is suspect, if only because my own
fairly prolonged frequentation of *The Secret Agent* has
failed to discover even one 'Anarchist young lady' in it to
whom Conrad might have been introduced.

Ford was probably thinking of his cousins, Helen and
Olivia Rossetti. They did write a fictional memoir of
their experiences as editors of an anarchist paper, *The
Torch*, under the title *A Girl Among the Anarchists*, by
Isabel Meredith (London, 1903). It gave, among other
things, a thinly disguised account of the Greenwich explosion. The account is very close to Nicoll's as regards
the role of Samuels (called Jacob Myers), and the supply-
ing of sulphuric acid to Bourdin (called Augustin Myers)
by Samuels from an anarchist called Dr Armitage, a
Harley Street doctor (Macdonald in Nicoll). In 'Isabel

Meredith's' account, however, Myers, the Verloc figure, accompanied by his wife, actually escapes to France to avoid giving evidence in the trial of two anarchists who are falsely accused of complicity in the outrage, and sentenced to five years' penal servitude.[8]

In *A Girl Among the Anarchists*, according to William Michael Rossetti, his daughters gave 'with fancy names and some modification of details, a genuine account of their experiences'.[9] Their account certainly tends to cast doubt on most of Ford's version where it differs from Nicoll's, except in two matters: Bourdin is shown as a rather simple enthusiast wholly under his brother's influence; and the brother's motives are suspect, though mainly for advocating irresponsible violence.

There is, then, no secure evidence for seeing Conrad's Verloc as being modelled on the historical Bourdin's brother or brother-in-law. Nor is it easy to find much beyond circumstantial evidence that the British Government of the period employed a secret informer who was both an anarchist leader and an *agent provocateur* for a foreign power. The general history of spying, however, shows that finding as many paymasters as possible is common, both among its important practitioners and even more among such marginal operatives as Verloc. Apart from Coulon there was another fairly close analogue to Verloc operating in London in 1895, Eugène Cottin, a French police spy pretending to be an anarchist. Cottin does not seem to have worked with the London police, however, and so his case only supports the general probability that since the communist and anarchist movements were international, and since England provided their main haven, foreign governments presumably met the threat in their usual ways. Thus the great outburst of terrorism in France from 1892 to 1895 probably explains the presence of both French anarchists and secret police agents in London which is often referred to by the press during the period.

The years between the Greenwich explosion and the writing of *The Secret Agent* were certainly the golden age of political *agents provocateurs*. The most picturesque example is that of the Russian Azev. On behalf of the Russian secret police he infiltrated the Socialist Revolutionary Party, became the head of its terrorist section, and there provided himself with impeccable subversive credentials by being involved in the assassination both of the Russian Minister of the Interior in 1904, and of the Grand Duke Sergei in 1905.[10]

Ford made Azev the instigator of Bourdin in two memoirs written long after Conrad's death. His most explicit account is in *Return to Yesterday*, and the passage is worth quoting at length for its no doubt over-coloured picture of the atmosphere surrounding the Russian anarchists and police in London at the time :

the fact that England was the international refuge for all exiles was not agreeable to the Russian police who filled the country with an incredible number of spies. There must have been at least one for every political exile and the annoyance that they caused in the country was extreme. I remember between 1893 and 1894 going home for longish periods almost every night from London University to a western suburb with Stepniak, Volkhovsky or Prince Kropotkin who were then the most prominent members of the Russian extreme Left and who were lecturing at the university on political economy, Russian literature and, I think, biology respectively. And behind us always lurked or dodged the Russian spies allotted to each of those distinguished lecturers. Stepniak or Volkhovsky dismissed them at Hammersmith station, as often as not with the price of a pint, for the poor devils were miserably paid, and also because, the spies and their purpose being perfectly well known in the district where the Russians lived, they were apt to receive very rough handling from the residents who resented their presences as an insult to the country. One or two quite considerable riots were thus caused in the neighbourhoods of Hammersmith proper and Ealing.

Those matters caused at one time a very considerable friction between the British and the Russian courts. The redoubtable Azev, who was the Russian chief spy-master and *agent provocateur*, conceived the fantastic idea that an outrage in England might induce the British Government and British public opinion to decree the expulsion of all political exiles from their shores, the exiles themselves being remarkably law-abiding. He accordingly persuaded a half-witted youth to throw a bomb into Greenwich Observatory. The boy, however, stumbling over a tree-stump in the Observatory Park was blown to pieces and the whole matter came to light. For diplomatic reasons, the newspapers made very little of it. But the Home Secretary, Sir William Vernon Harcourt, made such caustic remarks over it to the Russian First Secretary of Embassy that Russian activities on the Afghan border became very marked for a considerable period.

I happen accidentally to know a good deal of these episodes. My own house was once – and my mother's twice – burgled by emissaries of the Russian Embassy in search of documents. In my case, I being the owner of *The English Review*, the above-mentioned scoundrel Azev sent me by one of his emissaries a volume of the diary of the late Tzar; he imagining that I might like to publish it – which I didn't. I didn't want to have it in my house for more than a minute and took it round to my bank for internment whilst I informed the police. In the interval between then and my return, a little after midnight my house had been carefully gone through and all my papers, which were very many, had been thrown all over the floor. In my mother's case, the same thing happened twice, during the time that Father Gapon, the heroic leader of the peasants to the Tzar's palace on Bloody Sunday, was being housed by her, my mother being very charitable but by no means interested in politics. Eventually Gapon was sandbagged outside the house and the burglar – a Russian – given a long term of imprisonment. The Embassy naturally denied all knowledge of or responsibility for him. I came in that way a good deal in contact with the Scotland Yard Inspector who had charge of that sort of case and he told me a great deal about not only the activities of the Russian spies but gave me an – I daresay highly coloured – account of what the Home Secretary had said to the Secretary of the Embassy...[11]

In *Portraits from Life* Ford is briefer, but his account is important for its explicitness about how he supplied Conrad with the material on revolutionaries for *The Secret Agent* :

. . . *The Secret Agent* represents the anarchist-communists of London as being a pretty measly set of imbeciles, but it represents the *agent provocateur* – whom I knew well – as even more loathsome than the hideous Azev really was and the employer of that sad scoundrel as even more imbecile, if more sophisticated, than the shadows of Kropotkin, Stepniak, Volkhovsky, Bakunin, and the rest. And he had really made efforts to get behind the revolutionary mind. I supplied him with most of the material of that sort of book, and it was instructive in the extreme to see him react to those accounts of revolutionary activities. . . .[12]

Both passages date from the 1930s, long after the events described; and they are demonstrably unreliable in some important matters. Asquith, not Harcourt, was Home Secretary at the time of the Greenwich explosion; and Ford's relationship with Azev, even by his own account, belongs to the period when he was owner of the *English Review*, that is, not before 1908, two years after Conrad wrote *The Secret Agent*, fourteen after the Greenwich explosion, and in the same year that Azev was finally exposed in a Russian revolutionary review, and forced to go into exile. Ford elsewhere allows for the difference of dates when, after an account of his connection with the anarchist paper *The Torch*, he writes in *Return to Yesterday* that the association

had one other curious literary offshoot. That was *The Secret Agent* by Joseph Conrad. In one of my visits to *The Torch* office I heard the inner story of the Greenwich Observatory outrage. It was subsequently confirmed and supplemented to me by Inspector French of Scotland Yard after first my mother's and then my own house had been burgled by a professional cracksman employed by the Russian Embassy. I happened to tell the story to Conrad shortly after my burglary and, since he detested all Russians, and the Russian Secret Police in particular, he made his novel out of it. In his attribution to me of the plot which will be found in the Preface to the book he says he is sure that the highly superior person who told him the tale could never have come into contact with Anarchists. I have recounted above how I did.[13]

Ford fairly obviously conflated three different periods : that of the Greenwich explosion; that immediately before the composition of *The Secret Agent* (Bloody Sunday, in which Father Gapon was involved, occurred on 22 January ,1905); and that of Azev's exposure some years later. There are no doubt relics of the conflation of the first two periods in *The Secret Agent*; and so we must accept Ford's accounts as important sources for *The Secret Agent*, even if they are not accurate either as historical fact or as to what Ford actually told Conrad at any given time.[14]

As regards historical fact, for instance, the most convincing new detail in the last passage is highly dubious.

The official reticence of Scotland Yard has so far yielded to the importunities of scholarship as to inform me that 'I am directed by the Commissioner to say that, on the particulars supplied, it has not been possible to identify Inspector French as having served at Scotland Yard'.[15]

For the purpose of estimating what Ford told Conrad before *The Secret Agent* was written, the version of the Greenwich affair given in Ford's earliest mention, the 1911 *Ancient Lights*, is probably the best guide. In it neither Azev nor the Russian Government is identified; but the Greenwich explosion is already seen as a foreign effort to force the British Government to stop harbouring revolutionaries:

I don't know where the crowds came from that supported us as anarchists, but I have seldom seen a crowd so great as that which attended the funeral of the poor idiot who blew himself to pieces in the attempt on Greenwich Observatory. This was, of course, an attempt fomented by the police agents of a foreign state with a view to forcing the hand of the British Government . . . so that they would arrest wholesale every anarchist in Great Britain. Of course the British Government did nothing of the sort. . . .[16]

Again Ford erred. The new Tory Government did something of the sort by introducing a new Aliens Bill, and raiding the main anarchist meeting-places, the Autonomie Club and the office of *The Torch*. On the other hand the newspapers, and Nicoll's pamphlets, show that many anarchists agreed with Ford in thinking that the explosion was the work of an *agent provocateur* whose masters wanted to end the privileged asylum of foreign revolutionaries in England.

Conrad certainly had other sources besides Ford for the idea of secret but violent foreign interference in another country. He wrote in his letter to Cunninghame Graham of 7 October 1907 : 'Mr Vladimir was suggested to me by that scoundrel, General Seliwertsow, whom Padlewski shot (in Paris) in the '90s. There were peculiar circumstances in that case.'

General Seliverskov was a former Russian Minister of Police who was suspected of spying on Russian nihilists in Paris. Some of these were arrested by the French police when making explosives in a village near Paris in the May of 1890; and six months later Seliverskov was murdered in his hotel by a Pole, Padlewski, who was helped to escape by some revolutionary French socialists.[17]

The parallel to Vladimir is not, of course, very close; but Seliverskov at least is one example of a high Russian police official spying on anarchists in a foreign country. That this also went on in England can plausibly be inferred from the fact that the Russian Ambassador in London for many years, Count Shuvalov, had formerly been head of the Russian political police.[18] On the other hand, since the foreign anarchists in general did not want to jeopardise their safety in England, and since there were consequently very few examples of anarchist terrorism in England, the instigation of such activities as the Greenwich explosion by Russian or other foreign governments must be regarded as on the whole unlikely, or at least highly exceptional.

Whether Bourdin in fact intended a demonstration against the Greenwich Observatory, either independently, or under the instigation of genuine anarchists, irresponsible *agents provocateurs* such as Samuels, or even a foreign power, cannot now be determined. The choice of such a target would not in itself have been exceptional. Anarchist extremism preached public gestures against public institutions, and self-immolation added resonance

to the gesture. There is no anarchist parallel in England
to the Greenwich case, but the Fenians provide several.
Thus the Chicago Convention of 1886 determined to
mount 'a pyrotechnic display in honour of the Queen's
Jubilee' of 1887 – a projected dynamite explosion in Westminster Abbey; and in 1884 Mackay Lomasney was
blown to pieces by his own dynamite in a demonstration
against London Bridge.[19]

The Secret Agent, then, cannot be viewed as a reconstruction of the Greenwich explosion; and as regards
Conrad's claim to Methuen, echoing Ford's to him, that
it was 'based on the inside knowledge of a certain event
in the history of active anarchism', we can accept it only
with the proviso that, as we all know from reading the
newspapers, the inside story is often false. There are, however, reasonably close historical analogues for the novel's
general presentation of the activities of the anarchists,
the police, and the British and foreign governments: so
much so that, in his recent book *The Anarchists*, Joll
calls *The Secret Agent* 'the classic description of the relations between anarchists and police'.[20]

Where Conrad increases the distance between fact
and fiction is in two main areas. First, he creates a tighter
domestic drama. Ford seems to be responsible for making
Bourdin and therefore Stevie a half-wit, and for having
the Samuels or Verloc in the case murdered. Conrad may
have added the suicide of Winnie, though he was later
under the impression that he got it from Ford. These
changes also support the effect of the second and more
political kind of departure from the original circumstances. Adding Vladimir, and omitting any attractive,
impressive, or even merely English, revolutionaries,
tended to underline the irony of the picture, and to
deepen what Conrad called the 'criminal futility' of the
story. In short, although *The Secret Agent* is neither a his-

torical nor a Naturalistic novel, its distance from reality, though varying, is never very great. It takes an initiated, slightly fanciful, and above all very selective, view of the *milieu* and the events out of which the story arose.

It is the nature of this selective perspective which is the basis of Irving Howe's objection that *The Secret Agent* does not give a fair picture of the anarchist movement as a whole. And, of course, Conrad did not intend to. Nor need we see Conrad's perspective as merely an expression of his own conservative prejudices, since it was much more difficult for anyone then to see the positive significance of anarchism than it is now, either for Howe or for us.

Conrad had certainly been an arch-reactionary in his early days. In 1885, for instance, he wrote to a Polish friend, Spiridion Kliszczewski: 'Where's the man to stop the rush of social-democratic ideas? The opportunity and the day have come and are gone! Believe me: gone for ever. For the sun is set and the last barrier removed. England was the only barrier to the pressure of infernal doctrines born in continental back-slums. . . .'[21] As the years passed, however, Conrad's political views became less frenetic and more objective. As a Pole born under Russian occupation he remained anti-Russian, and of course in his day anarchism was largely a Russian movement; but by 1905, as his important political essay 'Autocracy and War' shows, Conrad had come to see Russian despotism and Prussian militarism as the main dangers to the European order. At this time, at least, the threat of revolution seemed much less so – and with good reason.

After the split between Marx and Bakunin, and the dissolution of the First International in 1876, the revolutionary movement split into many factions. As regards anarchism, the great traditions of Godwin and Proudhon,

continued by Bakunin and Kropotkin, were largely sub-
merged by the terrorist tactics of Nechaev. This dominance of *propagande par le fait* was confirmed in 1881
when a conference of revolutionaries in London, including Malatesta and Kropotkin, agreed that revolution
could only be brought about by illegal means. In the following decades anarchism was taken to mean terrorism;
and all Europe was in fact terrified. There were innumerable attempts on the lives of prominent statesmen
and royalty throughout Europe, and some were successful. Thus the assassinations of the Presidents of France
and the United States, of the Prime Minister of Spain, of
the Empress of Austria, of the King of Italy, were all
attributed to anarchists.

What was most striking in all this to Conrad, we can
assume, was the extraordinarily wide spectrum of persons
and motives which composed the anarchist movement and
its sympathisers. In every country they ranged from
high-minded sympathisers who were mainly concerned
with the degrading injustices of the current social order,
to the most marginal criminals and psychotics who sought
economic or emotional satisfaction in casual destruction.
Even within the official anarchist movement itself there
was a similar spectrum, from intellectual noblemen like
Kropotkin to ruthless fanatics like Johann Most.

Conrad was in France at the height of the terrorist
campaign early in 1894. There Vaillant, who had thrown
a bomb into the Chamber of Deputies, was condemned to
the guillotine despite the fact that no one had been killed.
President Sadi Carnot refused clemency, and as he died
Vaillant exclaimed: 'Long live Anarchy! My death
will be avenged.' It was indeed, for on 24 June 1894 an
Italian anarchist, Caserio, stabbed Carnot to death. In
the ensuing prosecutions the wide following of the anarchists received great publicity. The writer Félix Fénéon, a

civil servant in the Ministry of War, was prosecuted for forming a criminal association; and the subscription list of the main anarchist paper, *Le Révolté*, was found to contain the names of some of the most famous writers and artists of the day – France, Daudet, Leconte de Lisle, Signac, Seurat, Pissarro. When Mallarmé, who testified on Fénéon's behalf, was asked for his views on terrorism, he answered that 'he could not discuss the acts of these saints'.[22]

Anarchism had a similarly broad spectrum of adherents and sympathisers in England, from eminent intellectuals to the most feckless hangers-on. William Morris and Bernard Shaw were active supporters in the early 1890s; but it was difficult then to see what would come out of all the quarrelsome meetings and violent speeches. In some countries, as in Spain, anarchism was to become a viable tradition; in others, as in England, France and Russia, it was but one of many forces of protest which led to the creation and eventual victory of powerful socialist or communist parties. Many of the English anarchist sympathisers were concerned, in 1893, with the foundation of the Independent Labour Party; thirty years later one of its founding members, Ramsay MacDonald, would form the first Labour Government, and offer Conrad a knighthood.

Conrad, in *The Secret Agent* at least, seems blind to this historical perspective. One reason is probably that the political views and connections of his own immediate circle seemed to illustrate something that was both typical of the anarchist movement and very near to his own central concerns as a writer. The most aristocratic of his friends, Robert Cunninghame Graham, descended from the royal house of Scotland, and an M.P., had spent six weeks in jail for 'assault of the police' when the authorities broke up a Trafalgar Square meeting of the

Social Democratic Federation in 1887, which Kropotkin had also attended. Edward Garnett, a socialist, had
a similarly varied set of connections: his father was an
establishment figure, Principal Librarian of the British
Museum; while his wife, Constance, was friendly not
only with Kropotkin but with Stepniak, on whose behalf
she went on secret business to Russia not knowing that
Stepniak had earlier been a terrorist there and stabbed
General Mezentzev.[23] In his youth Ford himself had
been an anarchist; his sister married a Russian, David
Soskice, who had recovered from his Siberian exile in
the Garnetts' country home;[24] and most striking of all,
Ford's mother's half-sister, though the wife of William
Michael Rossetti, Secretary to the Board of Inland Re-
venue, nevertheless allowed her daughters to edit an anarchist journal, *The Torch*, in her own house.[25]

When Conrad, then, began to think about the tale
which was to become *The Secret Agent*, he had already
had close personal experience of the interpenetration of
order and anarchy in the political and social order. That
general conflict, together with individual isolation, were
already his chosen themes; and they combined to provide
an ironic perspective very different from the one in which
secret agents were usually viewed. For Conrad we are all,
one way or another, like Verloc: a little less conscious,
no doubt, and a little less venal, but still secret agents
torn between protecting and destroying the established
order. Society seems unaware of the problem; but then
society is really one vast conspiracy of blindness.

The fact that his locale was English, however, raised
personal problems of a peculiar complexity for Conrad.
Like the anarchists, he was himself a refugee from political
oppression and, deeply grateful to England as he was,
we may surmise that his elaborate notion of decorum
made him averse to any direct political criticism of his

adopted country. That there are no English anarchists in *The Secret Agent*, and that the anarchist theme is hardly allowed to have any serious domestic implications, may perhaps be regarded as in part an ironic tribute to his new country and his friends there. Unlike Conrad, neither his fictional English characters, nor his actual friends, seem able to imagine that there could conceivably be any serious threat to the continuance of their national life : in their insular security they treat politics as a game where, in the words of Sir Robert Anderson, 'the rules of the prize ring are held to apply to the struggle between the law and those who break it'.[26] In his heart, Conrad probably believed that trusting in such rules was just another example of Winnie Verloc's distaste for looking into things too deeply; but with courteous reticence he only said it in the most indirect and jesting way.

NOTES

1. Jean-Aubry, *Life and Letters*, ii 60. Conrad made several other similar denials. 'I know almost nothing of the philosophy, and nothing at all of the men', Conrad wrote in 1912 (*Letters of Joseph Conrad to Marguerite Poradowska, 1890–1920*, ed. John A. Gee and Paul J. Sturm (New Haven, 1940) p. 116); see also Elbridge L. Adams, *Joseph Conrad: The Man* (New York, 1925) p. 55.

2. Jean-Aubry, *Life and Letters*, ii 322.

3. Sir Robert Anderson, *The Lighter Side of My Official Life* (London and New York, 1910) pp. 175–6.

4. Sir Robert Anderson, *Criminals and Crime: Some Facts and Suggestions* (London, 1907) pp. 87–8.

5. Sir Robert Anderson, *Sidelights of the Home Rule Movement* (London, 1907) pp. 150–1.

6. See also David Nicholl, *The Greenwich Mystery* (Sheffield, 1897; discussed pp. 217–23 above); Major Henri

Le Caron's memoir, *Twenty-five Years in the Secret Service: Recollections of a Spy* (London, 1892); and A. G. Gardiner, *The Life of Sir William Harcourt* (London, 1923) II 44–50.

7. *Joseph Conrad: A Personal Remembrance* (London, 1929) p. 231.

8. Op. cit., pp. 39–73. The two anarchists are called Banter and O'Flynn (Cantwell and Quinn in Nicoll). Conrad's short story 'The Informer' deals with the same *milieu*; see James Walton, 'Mr X's "Little Joke" : The Design of Conrad's "The Informer" ', *Studies in Short Fiction*, IV (1967) 322–33.

9. W. M. Rossetti, *Some Reminiscences* (London, 1906) p. 450.

10. See Boris Nikolajewsky, *Aseff the Spy* (New York, 1934).

11. Ford Madox Ford, *Return to Yesterday* (London, 1931) pp. 134–7.

12. Ford Madox Ford, *Portraits from ife* (Boston and New York, 1937) p. 66 (published in London in 1938 as *Mightier than the Sword*).

13. Ford, *Return to Yesterday*, p. 114.

14. The Azev case, for instance, was certainly a source of *Under Western Eyes* (1911); and Ford probably confused the details of his help on the two novels. The parallels are treated in Morton Dauwen Zabel's 'Introduction' to *Under Western Eyes* (New York, 1963).

15. Letter from The Secretary, New Scotland Yard, of 10 October 1960.

16. Ford Madox Ford, under the title *Memories and Impressions* (London and New York, 1911) pp. 135–7. Sherry suggests a different view of the funeral (p. 218 and p. 228 n. 8 above).

17. *The Times*, 20 and 25 Nov 1890.

18. See Anderson, *The Lighter Side of My Official Life*, pp. 246–8.

19. Anderson, *Sidelights on the Home Rule Movement*, pp. 284–5, 150.

20. James Joll, *The Anarchists* (London, 1964) p. 128.

21. Jean-Aubry, *Life and Letters*, 1 84.

22. Joll, *The Anarchists*, pp. 96–135.

23. David Garnett, *The Golden Echo* (London, 1954) pp. 10–14.

24. Ford, *Return to Yesterday*, p. 131.

25. Ibid., p. 112.

26. Anderson, *Sidelights on the Home Rule Movement*, p. 127.

SELECT BIBLIOGRAPHY

Jocelyn Baines, *Joseph Conrad: A Critical Biography* (London : Weidenfeld & Nicolson, 1960; New York : McGraw-Hill, 1960).

Edward Crankshaw, *Joseph Conrad: Some Aspects of the Art of the Novel* (London : John Lane, 1936).

Richard Curle, *Joseph Conrad and His Characters: A Study of Six Novels* (London : Heinemann, 1957; Fair Lawn, N.J. : Essential Books, 1958).

Harold E. Davis, 'Conrad's Revisions of *The Secret Agent* : A Study in Literary Impressionism', *Modern Language Quarterly*, xix (1958) 244–54.

Wilfred S. Dowden, 'The Illuminating Quality" : Imagery and Theme in *The Secret Agent*', *Rice Institute Pamphlet*, xlvii (1960) 17–33.

Ford Madox Ford, *Joseph Conrad: A Personal Remembrance* (London : Duckworth, 1924; Boston : Little, Brown, 1924). Excerpts in F. MacShane (ed.), *Critical Writings of Ford Madox Ford* (Bison : Univ. of Nebraska Press, 1964.

Elliott B. Gose Jr, ' "Cruel Devourer of the World's Light" : *The Secret Agent*', *Nineteenth-Century Fiction*, xv (June 1960) 39–51.

Leo Gurko, '*The Secret Agent* : Conrad's Dark Vision of Megalopolis', *Modern Fiction Studies*, iv (1958) 307–18; reproduced as ch. 10 in Gurko's *Joseph Conrad: Giant in Exile* (New York : Macmillan, 1962).

John Hagan Jr, 'The Design of Conrad's *The Secret Agent*',

Journal of English Literary History, XXII (June 1955) 148–64.

Eloise Knapp Hay, *The Political Novels of Joseph Conrad: A Critical Study* (Chicago and London : Chicago U.P., 1963).

Douglas Hewitt, *Conrad: A Reassessment* (Cambridge : Bowes & Bowes, 1952; Philadelphia : Dulfour Editions, 1953).

Norman Holland, 'Style as Character : *The Secret Agent*', *Modern Fiction Studies*, XII (1966), 221–31.

Frederick Karl, *A Reader's Guide to Joseph Conrad* (London : Thames & Hudson, 1960; New York : Noonday, 1960).

G. D. Klingopulos, 'The Criticism of Novels', *The Use of English*, III (June 1955) 85–90.

D. R. C. Marsh, 'Moral Judgments in *The Secret Agent*', *English Studies in Africa*, III (Mar 1960) 57–70.

Bernard C. Meyer, *Joseph Conrad: A Psychoanalytic Biography* (Princeton U.P., 1967).

Claire Rosenfeld, *Paradise of Snakes: An Archetypal Analysis of Conrad's Political Novels* (Chicago U.P., 1967).

Norman Sherry, *Conrad's Western World* (Cambridge : Cambridge U.P., 1971).

Robert W. Stallman, 'Time and *The Secret Agent*', *Texas Studies in Literature and Language*, I (1959); reprinted in *The Art of Joseph Conrad: A Critical Symposium*, ed. R. W. Stallman (East Lansing : Michigan State U.P., 1960) pp. 234–54.

James H. Walton, 'Conrad and Naturalism : *The Secret Agent*', *Texas Studies in Literature and Language*, X (1967) 289–301.

——, 'The Backgrounds of *The Secret Agent* by Joseph Conrad : A Biographical and Critical Study', unpublished dissertation, Northwestern University : Summary in *Dissertation Abstracts*, XXVII 2164A–5A.

Paul Wiley, *Conrad's Measure of Man* (Toronto : Burns & MacEachern; Madison : Univ. of Wisconsin Press, 1954).

NOTES ON CONTRIBUTORS

AVROM FLEISHMAN. Author of *Conrad's Politics: Community and Anarchy in the Fiction of Joseph Conrad* (1967) and *A Reading of Mansfield Park: An Essay in Critical Synthesis* (1967). Now teaching at Johns Hopkins University.

JOHN GALSWORTHY (1867–1933). Novelist and dramatist. Author of *The Forsyte Saga* (1906–21) and *A Modern Comedy* (1924–8).

ALBERT J. GUÉRARD. Author of *Thomas Hardy: The Novels and Stories* (1949), *André Gide* (1951) and *Conrad the Novelist* (1958). Now teaching at Stanford University.

IRVING HOWE. Author of *Sherwood Anderson* (1951), *William Faulkner: A Critical Study* (1952), *Politics and the Novel* (1936) and *Thomas Hardy* (1967). Now teaching at Hunter College of the City University of New York.

FRANK RAYMOND LEAVIS. Author of *The Great Tradition* (1948), *Revaluation: Tradition and Development in English Poetry* (1953) and *D. H. Lawrence, Novelist* (1955). Edited *Scrutiny*, and taught mainly at Cambridge University.

THOMAS MANN (1875–1955). German novelist and man of letters. Author of *Buddenbrooks* (1923), *The Magic Mountain* (1932), *Joseph and His Brothers* (1934) and many other novels.

J. HILLIS MILLER. Author of *Charles Dickens: The World of His Novels* (1958), *The Disappearance of God: Five Nineteenth-Century Writers* (1963) and *Poets of Reality: Six Twentieth-Century Writers* (1965). Now teaching at Yale University.

V. S. PRITCHETT. Novelist, short-story writer and critic. Author of *The Living Novel and Later Appreciations* (1964) and *The Working Novelist* (1965). Now resides in London.

NORMAN SHERRY. Author of *Conrad's Eastern World* (1966) and *Jane Austen* (1966). Now teaching at the University of Lancaster.

ROBERT D. SPECTOR. Author of *English Literary Periodicals and the Climate of Opinion during the Seven Years' War: Studies in English Literature* (1966). Now teaching at Long Island University.

IAN PIERRE WATT. Author of *The Rise of the Novel: Studies in Defoe, Richardson and Fielding* (1957), and many other eighteenth-century and modern studies. Now teaching at Stanford University.

INDEX

Characters in *The Secret Agent* are indicated in small capitals.